ALONE ACROSS THE PACIFIC OCEAN

by

ALEX BELLINI

WITH A FOREWORD BY

ROKO BELIC

8 TABLES OUTSIDE THE TEXT

First published in Italy in 2010 by Longanesi & Co. © Gruppo Editoriale Mauri Spagnol

The 5th Element Ltd

16A High Street

Thame, OX92BZ

UNITED KINGDOM

Book ISBN: 978-0-9576457-3-8

Find out more about the author online at www.alexbellini.com

Contents

Foreword by Roko Belic

Ocean to highway

Sydney, December 12, 2008
Aprica, Summer 2006
Trieste, Spring 2007
Trieste 2007: a year of preparation
Italy-Peru, Winter 2007
Lima, January 2008
Land, February 2008
Leaving behind the world of shadows, February 21, 2008
Land, March 2008
S 10° 34′ – W 96° 38′, March 2008
Land, summer 2008
S 11° 10′ – W 88° 38′, March 2008
Land, June 2008
S 12° 25′ – W 128° 07′, June 2008
Land, September 2008
S 12° 12′ – E 177° 58′, September 2008
Sydney, November 2008
S 26° 03′ – E 158° 26′, November 11, 2008
S 26° 27′ – E 160° 07′, December 2008
Land, December 12, 2008
New Castle, December 13, 2008
Aprica, December 12, 2009

Malibu, California - May 28, 2013

When I first heard about Alex Bellini and his ocean rowing adventures, I felt a strong connection to his story because in 2001 my father was lost at sea while rowing across the Atlantic Ocean. Before my father began his journey, a journalist asked him why he would attempt such a thing as rowing a boat single-handedly across an entire ocean. His response was "That is a question to which there is no answer."

Having grown up on the coast of Yugoslavia my father, Nenad Belic, had felt a strong connection to the sea. As a child he dreamed of being a merchant marine, traveling the world by boat and experiencing exotic lands. But little Nenad's dream was put on hold when he was 13 after an important talk he had with his own father. They discussed whether he should become a merchant marine or a doctor, as he was also interested in medicine. "If you become a doctor and in a few years you decide you don't like it," my grandfather said to him, "you will still be able to become a merchant marine. But if you become a merchant marine and then you don't like it, it will be impossible to become a doctor."

So my father went to medical school, moved to the U.S.A., and ended up heading the cardiology department of a major hospital in Chicago. His work was meaningful, and he enjoyed it immensely for decades. But his dream to travel the seas did not die. Around his 50th birthday an idea came to him to row across the Atlantic Ocean. It took another twelve years to realize that dream. In that time, he drew the basic design for a boat that was later professionally refined and built, he read maritime books and he trained on Lake Michigan, sometimes for weeks at a stretch. He equipped his little yellow row boat with solar panels, GPS systems and stuffed it with over thousand pounds of food and supplies. Then in May, 2001 he set off from Cape Cod and rowed toward the shores of Europe. At 62 he was the oldest person to attempt that voyage.

We spoke by satellite phone every two weeks and he invariably sounded ecstatic. He described encounters with sharks, giant turtles, and birds of all types - and he loved it. He described sunsets where the entire sky, horizon to horizon in all directions, was swirled with the colors of the rainbow. I had never heard him in such a state of bliss as during those phone calls.

After some delays caused by headwinds and currents, the journey that my father expected would take around three months had stretched to four and a half. When he had nearly reached his goal, just a few days from the coast of Ireland, the first storm of the hurricane season hit with winds up to 70mph and waves as high as four story buildings. At 10:30pm GMT on September 30th, the Royal Coast Guard received an emergency radio transmission. A rescue team flew by helicopter, in the middle of the night and against gale force winds, 230 miles out to sea. They located the emergency transmitter floating alone in the tumbling ocean, but there was no sign of my father or his boat. For a month the heroic search continued, involving hundreds of people who volunteered to look for the missing rower by boat, plane, and by scanning the ocean from the high cliffs of western Ireland.

It was then that I started to learn about the many tragedies at sea faced by the people of Ireland and coastal areas around the world. It is not uncommon to lose a dozen or more sailors and would-be rescuers in a single storm season. These people risk their lives fishing, working on oil rigs and doing other jobs to provide for their families. How was it possible, I wondered, that these same people were willing to take time out of their days and even risk their lives to look for someone who, it could be said, was on a joy ride – rowing the ocean just for the hell of it? When I inquired, the answer came back loud and clear: "We understand what it is like to be at sea. We admire that courage that puts a person in a boat, alone, with no propulsion system other than his own body and a couple of oars, and makes him attempt a crossing of thousands of miles. We want to see him return safely to his family and friends."

My father never phoned me again. About a month after he disappeared at sea a fisherman came across a little yellow row boat floating some 40 miles offshore. All of the contents of the boat had been stripped away by brutal waves. The body of the boatman was never recovered.

Though my father could not articulate why he wanted to row, the people who searched for him understood. When we learn about a person willingly facing a challenge so great that it threatens their life, it ignites something within us. Deep down we know that this spirit is what moved early humans around the globe to discover new lands. This is the spirit that goes out to explore the remotest jungles and outer space, and Mankind's potential. We push ourselves to find our limits and sometimes, by doing so, we acquire the ability to surpass those limits.

In his solo crossing of the Pacific Ocean in a row boat, Alex Bellini did not aim to collect facts and figures, or make a new geographical discovery, or offer a methodology of how the human species can progress. Perhaps, even, his journey elicits in us more questions than conclusions. But in taking off into that great blue wilderness, Bellini gets at what it means to be human, because what defines us as a species is not idleness but action, not fear but courage, not resignation but hope. Alex Bellini's story, like those of Ernest Shackleton, Roald Amundsen, Amelia Earhart, Tenzing Norgay and Edmund Hilary and other great adventurers, inspires us to dream. These explorers and their achievements remind us that we can achieve more than we had previously thought possible. Though we may not ultimately die for our dreams, Alex Bellini's story encourages us to live for them.

Roko Belic

Academy Award nominated filmmaker

Ocean to highway

They say that television is the place of the excessive, the extraordinary, the over-the-top. There we see monstrous people, improbable stories, whereas on radio we talk about normal people, the world of the ordinary, real life and its everyday matters. This is why radio is more effective and appealing than television, both to listen to and to make. There is a sea between the television of the incredible and the radio of the regular. Alex Bellini crossed that divide. Or that ocean, more precisely. In fact, he crossed two oceans, as he had already crossed another ocean a few years earlier. It seems that once you've rowed one ocean, alone, on a little boat the length of a compact minivan, you get the itch to do it again on another one. I guess you get a taste for it, and the temptation to go back for seconds is only natural. So you go to Peru, you cram your little boat with a ton of freeze-dried food and a cake, and say goodbye to your wife: "Don't worry, we'll see each other for Christmas, and we'll talk on the phone. I'll call you as soon as I'm offshore." A few strokes of your oars and you're off. You're off to an exceptional, extreme, impossible, epic, risky, dramatic adventure.

You're off to solitude, distance, the sea, and its storms. Alex Bellini told a bit of his story on the radio, every Friday around 7:10 PM, on a show that was very popular with the listeners of Radio2. Now he's telling his story here, in a much more complete version, as if this were all a "regular" matter. He tells it with his language, from his perspective, his anthropological approach of an extreme traveler, like a friend, or an office-mate. He tells about himself and talks about us. Together.

Like no one before him, Alex Bellini has managed to join the extreme and the everyday. Distance, isolation and solitude come together with community and familiarity. Thousands of miles from any inhabited place, months after his only encounter with other human beings, Alex managed to stay close, very close, to others. He was part of a community, together with all of those who followed him, supported him, wanted to know more, and show him that they were with him. He was a solitary traveler, more than even those of the 19th century, but alone in company, with a great mix of people, a community of kinship. He rowed alone, every day, but he brought thousands of people with him. Live. He did so a bit through the radio and a lot with the Internet. He told his story every day, skilled at changing perspective on each occasion, though it would seem his stories would have the same ingredients: sea, sun, oars. He answered every question of all his listeners. And I mean every question. Questions that truly ran the gamut, from the perception of God in the South Pacific to the use of sunscreen in that same sea. With his mountain-man's patience, he always answered even the silliest questions like those that extreme adventure seem to elicit from people who stay at home. When he got a bit tired of it, he merely commented that he wouldn't answer questions he'd already answered, saying so courteously; classiness like his is a rare thing.

Many of these silly questions were asked by us, on the radio. Because we can't help ourselves. But communication was made.

Between Alex in the Pacific Ocean, and Caterpillar's listeners, in their living rooms or stuck in traffic on the highway, inching along the few miles separating them from home, after work on a Friday afternoon. Two extremes that couldn't be further apart, yet, able to communicate, creating a traveling community. More traveling for Alex, despite the winds and currents; and less for those in their cars, stopped, stuck in jams. A comparison came to mind, with all due respect for Alex Bellini's courage: who is doing the crazier thing? Is it the guy in the middle of the ocean or the one trapped on the highway like he is every day?

Ultimately, Alex Bellini is the first traveler of the new generation, the first in a line of a new breed of Italian explorers, whose most illustrious predecessors include the likes of Walter Bonatti and Ambrogio Fogar. What Alex brought new to the game, which brings him an evolutionary leap ahead, building a new strand of DNA for extreme athletes, was his ability to take with him in his boat, on his adventure, thousands of enthusiastic supporters, through new technology (the Internet) and old (the radio). These people took part in his adventure from the inside and were involved in it in ways that would have been unimaginable five or ten years ago. No one in any field had ever managed to do so before. We could say that even more than his accomplishment itself, it is the way in which it was done that makes Alex Bellini not only the first Italian to have rowed across oceans, but the first in the world to have done so in "participatory solitude".

Alex set a new paradigm, on his own, without marketing managers, look stylists, or other such ridiculous excesses. He did it with the simplicity of someone who always finds his way home, whether in the middle of the ocean, or on the highway with our listeners.

In the midst of all this was a strange communication tool, the satellite telephone, Iridium. This extreme tool, Iridium (with its associations with the American army, from Iraq, Afghanistan, and journeys to the South Pole) has been domesticated and brought into our everyday lives.

Alex's wife, Francesca, called him one evening from a cafe in a square in Lavagna (a seaside city, not coincidentally). She asked him how it was going and wished him a good night, even if it's night in Italy and day in the southern hemisphere. With moving from time zone to time zone, we could never figure out if it was the day of the day before or that of the next day. It was one phone call among many that Francesca made to Alex, just like any of us might call our loved ones. With the naturalness of communication. Though perhaps a little more expensive when the bill came due.

We have gotten so used to Iridium's particular sound, the distortion of the voice from bouncing across the skies, that the voice of anyone using it becomes the voice of Alex Bellini for us. Just like what he is telling us here in this book.

Massimo Cirri, Filippo Solibello

Sydney, December 12, 2001

Just after nine in the morning, Australia suddenly appeared on the horizon. While my eyes drank in that long-sought land, the unexpected question popped into my mind of what would be left of this moment in ten or twenty years. Which feelings would survive the passage of time and which would be lost forever? Would I have a happy memory of it? Or would I end up wanting to go back in time and rewrite my history?

"Whatever happens in a person's life, good or bad, it is the best thing that can happen for that person in that moment." These words were at the end of the last text message my wife Francesca had sent me a few days earlier on my satellite phone. I had repeated them in my head over and over in these last hours and now I thought I was starting to see their deeper meaning. The disappointment that I had felt at first at having to stop so few miles short of the Australian coast had given way to a total, serene acceptance of my fate. Life can be so strange and unpredictable, I thought. It makes us go around and around and then it ends up taking us exactly to the place we had done everything to avoid.

Because the sea was very rough, the operations for transferring and attaching my boat to the *Katea* towboat took a long time and the help of much of the crew. As I was feeling quite weak, I helped little with these maneuvers. More than anything, I was confused, disoriented, like a rag doll tossed to and fro on the deck. I was brought below deck. A guy who looked a year or two older than me gave me underwear, a T-shirt and a pair of pants, showing me the bathroom where I could change. Was this a come-on or just a way of taking care of me? On another occasion, I might have asked him, joking about it, but right then it was hard to say even a single word. I stayed in the bathroom for a very long time. First, I looked at myself in the mirror with the shock of someone who has regained his sight suddenly and can hardly recognize himself, and then I got under the warm, relaxing stream of the shower. I had the feeling that the more water I let run over my body, the sooner I would be free of the armor I had worn to protect myself to survive what had happened at sea. A clean smell came off the new clothes in my hands, so good that I held them to my face for a long time before I put them on. My hips and legs were so thin that those pants seemed to hold air, and I had to keep them up with a cord tied around my waist. Cleaned up and refreshed, I sat at the table and ate with the whole crew. A thousand thoughts flew through my mind at lightening speed, but I couldn't catch hold of a single one.

In my logbook, I had written down every thought and sensation of that whole long captivity at sea. Fear that time could rob me of the pleasure of remembering had pushed me to write down every detail with meticulous care. But that day of December 12 was hard to describe. I was disoriented and very tired, but the thought that I would see Francesca again within a few hours kept me from sleeping.

Every three hours, the crew shifts changed on the tugboat and new crew-members got up from their berths. Some hopped in the shower. Others went straight for coffee and then replaced their crew-mates who went to rest. I got the impression that I had aroused some curiosity in them, but otherwise life on board went on as usual, despite my presence as this taciturn foreigner. I tried to lie down in the bunk that they had given me, more out of boredom than necessity, but there was no hope of sleep.

I went up a few times to the upper level, in the wheelhouse. I talked a bit with the captain, a quiet man with a long, red beard, focused on controlling that unruly horse that was his ship. He spoke without ever taking his eyes off the electronic equipment that gave off a faint blue light. The slow crawl of the conversation gave me the chance to look over the plethora of equipment, weather reports, and nautical charts that filled the room. Though my first impression of him hadn't been the best, as I had gotten the feeling that my being on the boat was a nuisance to him, that long night changed my mind. He was from Auckland. In his thirty years of service, he had sailed almost all of the world's seas. Each of his terse sentences, and each breath and silence between each word, gave me a tiny glimpse to let me imagine just a small part of the incredible things that this man had experienced. His calm, composed manner was in distinct contrast to the fury of the sea he sought to tame. His ways were reassuring, like those of an old wise man.

There was a mysterious power that kept my eyes glued to what I saw outside. Maybe it was the same power that had brought me this far. The water was a thick black crust scratched by the foamy waves. It was lifted again and again by the wind like desert dust, obstructing our vision for a few dozen yards. It was only at that very moment that I truly understood the huge risk I had taken crossing an ocean as vast as the Pacific in my little boat. In this storm, it would have been hard for even the most careful seaman to see my navigation light and avoid hitting me, all the more because no one would be expecting me. My mind went back to the many nights in the Atlantic when, lacking an adequate radar, I risked being struck by ships that crossed my path. The very thought of how close some got to me still sends cold chills down my spine.

I'd never in my life seen such a dark night. A single, powerful beam of light rent through the darkness and lit my boat being towed a few dozen yards away. It would disappear under the waves to reemerge a few seconds later. I would not have bet a single cent on it making it ashore unscathed. That sea could have swallowed it at any second. Before I could let myself be overwhelmed by the fear of losing it, I would go below deck and sit down for one more cup of coffee.

The night passed quickly and suddenly another day at sea had begun. It was a heavy, misty morning, one of those when you can feel the fog in your bones. I was so concentrated on looking ahead, searching for dry land, I hadn't even noticed the rain that had soaked me from head to toe. And then there it was. I could hardly believe that what I was looking at was Australia.

On my long journey begun in Peru, I had imagined its coastline so many times. I'd envisioned it high and rocky, yet lushly green. But now what I was looking at was gray sand and flat lines, just barely distinguishable from the sea. Scattered everywhere, like wrecks abandoned at sea, ships were anchored, awaiting authorization to enter the port.

I was filled with mounting impatience to walk on land again and see Francesca. Though it was still very windy, the sea's fury was calming. A cold rain was falling, making the air around me even heavier and thicker. With growing agitation, I watched the maneuvers of the *Katea*'s crew preparing to come into the harbor as a helicopter from Channel 7 filmed the scene from above. Only when I was quite close to the docking area did I glimpse a small group of people. The first to recognize me was Stefano. He and Roger had sent me weather forecasts almost daily. He was there to welcome me, just as he had been when I arrived in Fortaleza.

Standing apart from the group of people I then caught sight of Francesca, still in a corner, holding an umbrella and looking in my direction. Everything abruptly slowed down. In that fraction of an instant that seemed endless, I was ripped away by an irresistible force and my mind was taken back to two hundred and ninety-four days earlier in Lima, when, with my heart shattering, I watched her figure growing smaller and smaller until it disappeared on the horizon. A deep gash had opened in my heart and been filled by the sea over those ten months. A few excruciatingly slow seconds passed in which everything was motionless. Then Francesca raised her arm and shouted my name and that's all it took to start the world back up. That single word shouted under the rain hit me with the force of a hurricane and filled the void that months of solitude and silence had formed inside me.

It had been forty-two weeks since I had last seen my wife and forty days since I had last talked to her on the phone. Crossing the Pacific Ocean was like having crossed through our lives. Now we were together again and stronger than ever. I think that every seafarer needs two essential things on every journey: a lighthouse and an anchor. Francesca was both for me. In storms, she always showed me which way to go, and her love, understanding, and constant presence kept me from going adrift psychologically. One thing was certain. With all that enormity of water that we had together touched, drank, and experienced, nothing would ever be the same.

Aprica, Summer 2006

The first time I considered rowing across the Pacific was a few days after I had passed the Strait of Gibraltar on my Atlantic Ocean crossing. Before that, it had been nothing more than a vague notion, and I didn't think I could really handle it. Susceptible to the call of the sea, I saw that the infinite stretch of water had a magical pull on me. Just making the sound of the word, Pacific, started me buzzing and dreaming.

In 2005, my crossing from the Mediterranean to the Atlantic had plenty of difficulties and unplanned events. Repelled twice by powerful sea currents and grazed by three enormous container ships, I had started to think that I would never manage to pass the legendary "pillars of Hercules". Making matters worse, this time it wasn't just the sea throwing unexpected problems in my way. I also had quite an exceptional encounter with the Moroccan police. One morning, they came alongside me and chased me down. They thought I was a drug trafficker! They confiscated my passport and escorted me to the port of Tangiers, where I stayed for four days until the Italian consulate resolved the matter and I could go back to the sea. It was such an irony, as just forty days before, rowing between the Balearic Islands, I had fished a 65-pound suitcase full of drugs out of the sea. I got rid of it on the spot, sinking each pack in the sea one by one.

On December 7, I managed to leave the Mediterranean behind me and plunge into the immensity known as the Atlantic. Extremely difficult times lay ahead. Because of terrible sea conditions, for about eighteen days, I had to stay in my three foot by 6.5 foot cabin, without so much as being able to stretch my legs. In that tight space, I even grew short on air. These were among the worst moments of my life. To avoid drowning psychologically in that rough, dark water, I always tried to anchor myself, with all my strength, to a positive a thought, a new goal. I obsessively repeated the mantra: "Stay strong, Alex. Don't give up. Later, you'll do the Pacific!"

Picturing myself working on achieving another crossing was a huge help to me in the years after that as well. I'd called Roger and asked his opinion on when it was best to cross the Pacific Ocean. When he heard my question, he could hardly conceal his astonishment, "Doesn't what you're doing now seem enough?", but he gave me his opinion anyhow. After researching, he told me that February was the best time. Leaving in that period, the end of the summer in the southern hemisphere, I would be able to take advantage of very favorable weather conditions. If I reached Australia before the end of November, my arrival would be under good conditions.

Meanwhile, I was still in the Atlantic and the course yet to go to get to Brazil was truly long. At the time, I could have not even begun to imagine what was awaiting me on that long journey, all the challenges and fears I would have to face before setting foot on land again. Yet, even with all the problems and hard times I went through, there was not a single day in which I failed to think about the new ocean that seemed to be calling me from afar.

My 2006 trip had ended after two hundred and twenty-six days on the beach of Fortaleza, where the entire town welcomed me as a hero. This was the end of an adventure started two years earlier, with two failed attempts. I could at last enjoy the pleasant sensation of being full and complete. Going back home after almost eight months of solitude had been extremely emotional. More than pleased to have succeeded, I felt glad to have survived. My physical recovery was slow and took a good bit of patience. My body had been put under severe strain and needed special care. It wasn't until the end of the summer that I regained my strength. Psychologically, though I had been standing on land for some time, I felt like I had yet to touch ground, and I lived in something of a limbo.

Throughout 2006, I took part in many conferences and public events. Each time I met hundreds of people, many of whom had followed every step of my journey on the web site and on the radio. On my little boat, I never felt truly alone because I had the company of the dreams of hundreds, perhaps thousands, of people whose great energy I felt. It had been an adventure for the entire community that came together around me. More than anything, this huge success in communication had been cause for much pleasure and pride.

Despite all this attention and my desire to tell about my experience, there were many times that the need to immerse myself again in the sea felt stronger than what was keeping me on land.

What was it that was pushing me again towards the sea? What more could I, or did I want to find? Wondering about this urgency to go once again in the sea, which I felt as pleasurable and unbearable at once, I closed my eyes and tried to take my mind back to those days I spent alone. I felt an inexplicable pleasure in the feeling of disorientation triggered by the thought of the sea. It was the perfect place to experience the effect of the feelings of empty space and the lack of boundaries.

I'd say that the sea stands for the unconscious, depth, and mystery, which are things it has in common with the human soul. This is why they say that we find ourselves in the sea. The sea is an emblem of dynamic movement, a place where everything is created and renewed. It is also doubt, uncertainty, and a lack of solidity. This may be why many people fear it. I've never been afraid of water. In fact, my mother says that when I was little, her problem was keeping my sister and me out of the sea. I remember that I always came out of the water with blue lips and pruned skin. My favorite thing was to dive off of ever higher points. At the time, this was one of my greatest expressions of freedom.

It's no wonder that people still love going by sea. The sea joins the destinies of those it welcomes. When you come across other seafarers on your route, you feel like brothers. Going by sea to an invisible destination is the perfect representation (sometimes overused) of surpassing your limits, your boundaries. Driven by what has been called Ulysses Factor, a common denominator of the human species, people of every era have felt the desire to explore themselves by facing the unknown and going beyond it to find their answers and their roots. Deciding to take to the sea, you make a clean cut with your habits. Those who have ever tried to change their habits, whether for the short or long term, know that it's the hardest thing in the world. The open sea is the non-place where everything blurs. Its horizons are flat lines, boundaries to be surpassed, where everything appears in a new guise. Beyond the geographic boundaries, outside of our usual, familiar places, freed from mental restraints and social strictures. This lets you radically change your perspective on everything. Everything seems different, including yourself.

As soon as I was back on land, I realized I was madly in love with Francesca. A bit after I returned from the Atlantic, at the end of October, after only three months in a relationship, I asked her to marry me. Having asked her to become my wife, I decided to put an end to my instincts to explore myself through travel and to dedicate myself fully to the family that I so much wanted to create with her. I decided that being with a person meant staying physically close to that person and taking on all the responsibilities that this decision entailed. I was calm and sure. Marrying her was all I wanted in life. Almost eight years had gone by since I met her in Milan. From that very first moment, I felt a need to take care of her. Now I wanted to be the one to make her happy.

Deciding not to leave again was a decision I came to slowly and with difficulty. While I felt sure it was the best thing to do, it was an enormous sacrifice. One thing filled me with genuine terror if I were to go: the thought that distance could weaken our bond, and when I would come back to land, I would find that now I was too far from her. We'd always had the habit of talking together and discussing everything. When a while later I confided my fears to her, it was Francesca who encouraged me to go. She said that she would never accept being with a person who made the wrong decisions and risked regretting a missed chance. Having her as a wife is one of the greatest strokes of luck I've had. In May 2007, Francesca handed in her resignation from her job, and we were both able to work full time on organizing the project. Managing the press office, she took care of communications, relations with sponsors and the press as well as coordinating the land support team. She took on a lot of responsibility, but she had all the qualities to do an excellent job and took her work very seriously.

We got married on July 7, 2007 in Aprica, my hometown, on a gorgeous sunny day, surrounded by friends and the mountains. When it came time to exchange rings, I couldn't get the ring on her finger. What then? Impulsively, I licked her finger as the priest's eyes popped. This unexpected event made the guests burst into laughter. The festivities continued in a CAI mountain refuge, 6.000 ft above sea level, which was run at the time by one of my two best friend. We organized a picnic there. The perfect end to an incredible day. For our honeymoon, we chose to take the Santiago de Compostela pilgrimage route in Spain. That long journey, five hundred miles, from the Pyrenees to the Atlantic, taken by countless pilgrims since the Middle Ages, had long been among the many trips we dreamed of taking together. We found the idea of taking such a long journey together appealing and the perfect metaphor as a prologue for a much longer path that we would take together in our married life. The original (or least unusual) thing was how we chose to travel the five hundred miles: on a tandem bike built just for the purpose. It was such a wonderful trip! There was no shortage of difficulties, but the satisfactions were many more. Taking dusty paths, crossing new landscapes under the sun or heavy rain, falling and getting back up, finding shelter for the night, and setting off the next morning to discover new routes gave us the first great joys of our new married life. Though Francesca was never an exercise fanatic, she found that she loved cycling. When we got home, she bought a bicycle for herself. It was hilarious when a few nights after we got back, I saw her peddling her legs in her sleep (she denies it to this day.)

I'd met Francesca in 1999, during a training course in Milan, the same year as I lost my mother. Since then, every time I left, she was always there to encourage me and support me in my choices. Soon, she got in the habit of giving me a small object that I would give back when I returned. Giving me something of hers gave her the security that I would eventually come home, if only to keep the promise to give it back. During my second attempt at the Atlantic, she had given me the *Le Petit Prince* by Antoine de Saint-Exupery. That attempt ended abruptly after only twenty-three days with a shipwreck in the island of Formentera. Almost nothing was saved from the wreck, just some bits of the boat and a piece of an oar. The copy of *Le Petit Prince* was also lost to the sea with my boat. The next year I managed to buy a fiberglass boat from a German man who had attempted to cross the Atlantic a few months before. Cleaning it out of everything that had been left on board, hidden in a locker, I found a copy of the same book, sitting in a pool of water. It was a French edition exactly like the one I'd been given! Over the years, this episode led me to pay attention to all those events we like to call coincidences. They have tremendous importance for me and help me open my eyes to the life we live, which we don't always dictate. My relationship with Francesca has been punctuated by these kinds of coincidences, so many that they can't be just happenstance. These synchronicities make us feel that we can communicate at a higher level, an ability that we have found of great importance in this long story of ours.

Trieste, Spring 2007

From the first day I met him, we've had a wonderful friendship. Alex has always had eyes beaming with enthusiasm. He seemed to already have everything he needed to be happy, but he had a dream tucked away in his heart. We were opposite, with different dreams and ambitions. Mine were still influenced by my family upbringing, which didn't let me stake out my own place in the world. Alex's dreams were much freer to express themselves. Since his first adventure in Africa, at the Marathon des Sables across the Sahara, I've always deeply supported his adventures. For me, he was a happy island to take refuge in difficult times, and a land happily far from the influences of others. The heat, cold, and effort had left their marks on his hands and face. Those creases on his face were not the marks of time merely passing, but rather the marks of how he had decided to live his life.

After he got back from Brazil, his eyes were full of the sea and he often drifted off, even with people all around. In those moments, I knew he was already far away and nothing could be done to stop him. I knew well those silences, those distractions, and they told of untouched places he still wanted to explore. Though he'd said that he didn't want to go back to the sea for a long time, I knew that it was calling him back. That faraway voice was making itself heard to him again.

The beginning of our relationship had been full of the natural excitement of a new couple, and particularly of our constant desire to travel, a passion that had long connected us. We spent full days dreaming of taking a suitcase and wandering the world like two gypsies. We dreamed of buying a vehicle to be able to travel for at least two years. We had already started to devise a route with specific stops. Both of us chose six places to visit, the ice of the north, great expanses of desert, Tibet, Africa, the Amazon forest. We could choose any destination we wanted. I remember one evening when we ended up falling asleep in each other's arms, stretched over a map of the world. Right then I realized that that world somehow already belonged to us. Needless to say, it wasn't long before marriage was proposed. After having known each other through and through for eight years, we knew we were looking at the person with whom we wanted to spend the rest of our time on earth.

Making such an important decision, I accepted the idea of seeing him leave, some day, for who-knew-what destination. My job then would be to let him go, even if faraway, as this would be the only way to have him as I'd met him, thirsty for adventure and full of life. Then I got a call from him one evening. It had been a few days since he'd told my family he planned to marry me. "I've decided not to go anymore. It's the right thing for me to stay near you!" I didn't know what to say. He would have given everything up, all his dreams for me, for us, for our family.

We had talked a lot about future plans that would have had us both committed on land, side by side. We were full of ideas and we had joined our lives to start a new life. Having children, leaving Milan to find a quieter place, maybe in the mountains where he was born.

But Alex was changing before my eyes. I saw the light in him dim and he grew gloomy, and I guessed at the reasons. I had told him that whatever his decision was I would support him. I reminded him that love should never, for any reason, chain us; it should free us. I would have never wanted to fetter him and, most of all, I would never want him, years down the road, to regret a wrong decision. In other words, I was just asking him to keep on being himself and do everything to follow his dreams. I would always be by his side, whatever he decided to do.

It was the beginning of a new, beautiful adventure, and soon I learned that everything starts long before you actually leave.

Trieste 2007: a year of preparation

I had made so many mistakes in organizing my adventure in the Atlantic that it was lucky that I had come home safe and sound. I had filled my logbook with pages and pages of notes, most of which had to do with food. I'd underestimated the consequences of a diet that didn't fit my caloric needs. This was compounded by problems caused by the repeated flooding of the lockers that made much of my food stores rot before I got to my destination. I'd put myself in serious danger. Some of these problems, like my gums receding due to the long lack of vitamin C, will be irritations that I will have with me for the rest of my life. For this new crossing, I wasn't willing to suffer the same problems. Of essential importance was the support I received from many individuals who helped me implement my plan, both organizationally, and, most importantly, for my diet.

Roger, Stefano, and Cristiano had agreed to be part of my support team again as they had been for the first crossing. Roger and Stefano were again in charge of getting me information about weather conditions and suggesting the best course to take. Roger never played just one role. Wherever there was a problem, he got in there and fixed it. He loves new technology, the Internet, and communication, and was essential for helping search the market for the equipment best suiting my needs. Stefano's day job is communication's director at Findomestic, and he's an expert sailor. On very many occasions, he gave me excellent advice to solve all kinds of unexpected problems on board.

Supporting Roger and Stefano, a new person had joined the team named Rick Shema, a highly skilled solitary Hawaiian sailor and meteorology expert. His deep knowledge of that vast ocean was an extra assurance for me.

Cristiano was the webmaster and took care of the technical aspects of telecommunications between the ocean and the web, making sure the web site worked. At some points in the adventure, the site was visited by thousands of people daily.

The land planning took a long time and a lot of care. Planning the period to do the crossing and finding the best time to leave were very sensitive. The success of the entire crossing could depend on it, and, really, so could my life. First, we estimated the duration of the crossing. With an average of thirty miles a day, the Pacific could be crossed in between eight to nine months. According to Rick Shema's advice, the end of December would be the latest I should arrive in Australia, because the start of the year is also the start of the hurricane season, and it would be ill-advised to be at sea then. If December was the deadline for arriving, then mid February was the best time to leave. February also seemed the perfect month to leave because it promised quite stable weather conditions.

The boat, after long months in my friend Alessandro's shed, had been moved to Trieste, where Francesca and I moved after the wedding. I'd entrusted it to a company well-known in the boating industry for its professionalism and this choice proved decisive. Major work was needed to repair its electric system, which had been damaged in my Atlantic crossing. Two parallel electric systems had been built, independent from each other, so that if the main one broke down, I could rely on the secondary one. Their absorption capacity was also raised by installing seven solar modules, divided into rigid and flexible panels. The greater amount of electric power available let me install a new radar device called AIS, automatic identification system. This device provided both the regular services of a radar and the name, origin, direction, and cruising speed of any ship in a five-mile radius. It was also able to signal my position on the radars of these ships, giving me a big safety advantage.

My boat had been repainted from top to bottom with special care for the hull on which I had applied an excellent antifouling paint. During the first crossing, I'd had a lot of problems with plant life growing on the boat's underwater part, which slowed me down a lot. I thought of the hull and antifouling paint day and night and it soon became my main fixation. I wanted to find a permanent solution and I hoped that I wouldn't be forced to dive underwater occasionally to remove the encrustations from the boat's surface.

The big difference between this adventure and the last one was in my psychological, physical, and dietary preparedness. Dr. Giulio Rossi, director of the Center for Sports medicine at the Morelli hospital in Sondalo performed all needed physical tests, assessments, and evaluations of physiological parameters. Based on these exams, Dr. Zoia, an expert in sports nutrition, calculated my daily energy need to sufficiently handle extended exertion. He calculated a daily diet of about 3,400 kilocalories. The main problem was the small space available for the galley and the length of the crossing. Ultimately, we managed to squeeze a food supply that would last for 350 days on the boat. My diet would be based on natural foods. Of course, I would have to have freeze-dried, precooked meals that could meet the two most important requirements: lasting long and taking up little space. Three days of the week, my main meal would be a special pasta designed and tried out with cross-country skiers, biathletes and short track athletes. This was a food made with a mixture of different flours, all organic, including durum wheat flour, wheat germ, rice, soybeans, chickpeas, oats, walnuts, and almonds, in the right doses to make a perfectly balanced food, both in quantity and in the quality of its nutrients. Topped with extra virgin olive oil and a bit of freeze-dried Parmesan cheese, it would be an excellent food that could give my body the optimal amount of proteins, fats, carbohydrates, minerals, and vitamins. There was still the problem of Vitamin C, which is found mainly in fresh produce. After meticulous research, Dr. Zoia had gotten me about 65 pounds of freeze-dried fruit, bananas, peaches, pears, kiwi and pineapple, that were made with a process the preserved much of their vitamins, including Vitamin C. With a daily ration of about 0.35 ounces of freeze-dried fruit, I would be able to prevent the problems caused by the lack of vitamins such as those that often dogged seafarers of past eras. Dr. Zoia had also formulated and had made especially for my needs two varieties of biscuits with high nutritional value: a sweet cookie based on almonds, and a salty biscuit with Parmesan cheese. These delicious biscuits were the foundations of my snacks.

The biofeedback training sessions with Dr. Rossi were of great help. I had never had biofeedback training sessions before, but my earlier experiences had helped me develop simple techniques to find concentration, inner quiet, and general relaxation. By controlling their bodies through breath and thought, free divers can stay underwater without breathing for dozens of minutes. Such performances are clear proof of the potential of the human mind.

When I'd finished work on the boat a few weeks behind schedule in late October, with less than two months to go until the date set for departure, I started training in the sea again. With increasing frequency, at least twice a month, I had to go to Valtellina to undergo new assessment tests at the hospital in Sondalo and at Dr. Zoia's office. At the end of November, we began the long process of packing all of the food in single-portion, vacuum packs. Francesca and her mother had spent almost every evening through Christmas packing hundreds of pounds of provisions. Our little apartment in Sistiana had quickly become a warehouse of stacked boxes, so many that we even had to keep them in our bedroom. Soon our house was a disaster area and we started to feel a sense of displacement looking at the spectacle.

By December 24, the boat had to be ready and loaded with everything to be transported to Genoa, from which it would make its way to Peru. That unmovable deadline had forced us to work our hardest, and sometimes was a cause of stress and conflict. No question that the real adventure would be getting to the departure safe and sound, which now and then seemed an impossible task. Rowing across the ocean would be child's play in comparison. Everything would be simpler once I set off from Lima. We were so busy organizing my departure that I hadn't even stopped to consider the psychological implications of being away from home for such a long time.

It was hard to breathe when I thought about it, but I'd decided that I would handle it when the moment was right and I'd get through it one way or another. I talked about it often with Francesca and admitted my worries. Soon life at sea would have me immersed in a new world that would require total concentration. There wouldn't be space or time for memories and homesickness. She always answered me very firmly. We had decided to embark on this project together. Together, we had considered all the pros and cons, and together, we would take it all on with total peace of mind. Of course, we were well aware that we were about to start a fantastic adventure that would teach both of us a great deal.

Finally, it came time to leave. On January 10, we got on a direct flight to Lima. The moment of getting up on that dark, cold morning was one of excitement, huge expectations, as well as sadness. Seeing the ground sliding beneath me, I thought how much time would go by before I saw that land again and how many things might happen before then…

Italy-Peru, Winter 2007

As the days went by, the project took shape. We had decided to live in the present and not think too much about the moment of separation, which, though we knew it was still far off, caused us both pain. I often observed Alex, absorbed in his thoughts while he was taking an inventory or making a repair to the boat. I would catch his eyes and see that he was anxious, but when I would ask what was wrong, he would say he was just a bit tired. Come on! He was my husband. I knew him extremely well and knew he was lying. I wanted to tell him not to worry, that I would be fine. But talking about it would have opened a gaping hole in our hearts. I sensed he was feeling a sense of urgency. I knew he was afraid I would feel alone and lost during his absence. I, on the other hand, was worried for him, as I would be surrounded by countless distractions, my family, our friends, and Dusty, our little greyhound. Alex would be alone in the middle of the ocean. He would have to face his fears day after day in solitude.

But we felt ready to handle any situation. This was all possible because we both believed in it deeply.

In the last days before the boat's departure for Lima, the tension was so high that any little thing could make our nerves flare, and we had our little spats. Christmas Eve was the last time we had really celebrated, as the boat had been loaded on the container direct to South America. After a gourmet dinner, we had gone back to our little home together. We were, and always would be, one entity, even with an ocean between us.

On January 10, at five in the morning, we left from the Venice airport for Lima. We hadn't even gone to sleep at all that night. We found ourselves packing at the last minute. On the trip from Trieste to the airport, I made a huge effort to avoid falling asleep, to keep Alex company while he drove. Once we got to the airport and checked in, we fell asleep on the waiting room chairs. The speaker called our names and we woke with a start. The waiting room was empty. Still sleep dazed, we grabbed our hand luggage and went to the boarding area. The ground under us quickly disappeared and we were soon wrapped in clouds. At long last!

Lima, January 2008

After a long journey, almost fourteen hours long, we landed in the airport of Lima, where it was already nighttime. The air was hot and heavy, but gusts of fresh wind from the ocean pleasantly cooled the atmosphere. The humidity, which condensed on the airport windows and caressed my skin during those first steps on Peruvian soil, was my first contact with the Pacific on this adventure. Waiting at the exit was an Italian friend who lived in Peru, Mario Lovati, whom I had met by Internet a few months earlier. Around the end of October, he had gotten into contact with us and offered to help us find a place to stay and take on the intricate mazes of local bureaucracy. Peru gave us a rather rude welcome. Because of the exhaustion from the long trip from Italy, helped along by a bit of chronic forgetfulness, I got off the airplane and forgot in my seat pocket a folder with about three thousand euros in cash in it. By time I realized that I'd left it on the plane, I was already in line waiting from my turn at immigration. I went back down the long corridor to the entrance of the plane, but the police immediately stopped me. When I tried to explain why I needed to get back on board, I was relieved by their understanding and support. They seemed to really want to help me solve the problem. They wrote down my seat number and asked me to wait while they went to check. I was sure that they would soon find the money because we had been the last to get off the airplane. But I never saw the police officers or the folder of money again. I was furious, indignant, and felt a huge sense of shame. I sure hadn't got off to a good start. All of the excitement and enthusiasm I had when I left Italy for this country waiting to be discovered had slipped away. I didn't even know what I was doing here.

Bright and early the next morning, to lighten the still tense atmosphere, we threw ourselves in the midst of the city's chaos.

We wandered the streets to look for our first experiences of Peru. We were overwhelmed by sharp odors, rubber and smog, mixed with the smells of multicolored ways of life, food, and hot asphalt. There was a blur of people everywhere on foot, cars, and buses, so bursting with people they seemed ready to explode. Though this was one of the best residential areas of Lima, there was a great confusion and a multitude of sensations from that first day that I still can't convey in words. The enormous rift between the rich and the poor was on clear display everywhere. There was nothing in between. On every corner of the street, the gap was glaring, with the two extremes clashing, like I'd seen before in Fortaleza.

The prestigious Club de Regattas in Lima, the most important boating club in all of South America, was interested in my project. Thanks to the support of the sports area manager, we had been made temporary members and enjoyed special treatment. The club is south of Lima, at the base of a hill on which one of the city's many poor neighborhoods was located. They had given me use of a small garage and a fenced area where I could keep the boat until my departure, planned from an adjacent pier. A cement wall separated the Club de Regattas' property from the public beach. On this side of the wall, beach umbrellas and lounge chairs were lined up with such order, they seemed to have been drawn with a ruler. In a relaxed setting, Peruvian women bustled back and forth in white aprons, taking care of the members' children. Its many restaurants served excellent food at decidedly high prices. On the other side of the wall was the rest of Peru. A chaotic heap of people and colors; men, women, and children squeezed so close together that you couldn't see the color of the sand under them. A huge blanket of smog and smoke seemed to hang over them, making it an even more dispiriting sight.

After the first days that we'd spent visiting the city like any two tourists, we were almost completely consumed by customs' procedures that, at points, seemed impossible to get through. We constantly had the feeling that we weren't being understood. Soon we realized that this was just a strategy. Patiently, we had to take it all patiently, with what we nicknamed the "*cinco minutinos*" attitude. Corruption made it useless to try to solve problems in the usual way (with words), and we often had to come in with cash in hand.

But everything has its limits. We weren't willing to accept compromises that were often on the edges of legality. The container ship that had carried my boat was stuck for two weeks in the port of Lima awaiting authorization to enter and was docked only in early February. We had already made an agreement with the company to help us with the customs' procedures then. We waited impatiently to be able to go get it. In the morning, we'd wake up sure that that was the day it would happen, but the days always ended with empty hands. Every single time we seemed close to a solution, the delivery company asked for new documents, payments, and endless lists of authorizations to show the custom's agent. We couldn't take it anymore. This arm wrestling had become exhausting. The day that the agency informed us that, to get the boat out of customs, we had to deposit a sum equaling its commercial value at a local bank, ensuring that it was a temporary import, Francesca and I looked into each other's disheartened eyes. A chilling silence fell between us. It was just a second, but I swear that for a sliver of a moment I thought it was all over. Even the Italian Embassy and the ambassador himself had come to help us, but it seemed we really had to deposit the sum of about 30.000 euro, as the Peruvian government didn't believe the story of the adventure. They were afraid I wanted to resell it without paying the import taxes! From Valtellina in Italy, the Banca Popolare of Sondrio said it would be able to deposit the money. But then we still had a problem because it would take at least a week, which we couldn't afford to wait. Meanwhile, completely unbeknownst to us, Roger had contacted all the Italian associations in Peru and one day he got a phone call from Renzo Lercari, president of the Association of Ligurians in Peru. It seems he was someone with the right connections. Just twenty-four hours after we first heard from him, we were able to go to the port of Callao and get the boat. We were escorted by armed men, Renzo's friends because of the danger of kidnapping or mugging. It felt like being in the middle of the Wild West.

Having solved the main problem, there was still a not insignificant detail that needed our total attention. For the success of the adventure, we needed to choose the best date to leave with the least possible margin of error. In an ironic twist, the success of a crossing that is more than nine thousand miles was all about the first hundred miles. It was unbelievable. There were many factors to consider.

On one hand, the particular wind and current conditions near the shore pushed masses of cold water north throughout the year coming directly from the Antarctic. Their particular intensity would have certainly caused problems for my crossing. On the other hand, there was the need to have a correct navigation strategy to stay towards the mid-latitudes as much as possible. Between ten and twelve degrees south, to be able to pass the dense network of cays that make up French Polynesia, in natural passageway between the Tuamotu Islands to the south and the Marquesas Islands to the north. If we made the wrong decision, the risk was that I would be pushed off course northwest by the current and get too close to the Galapagos Islands, which would be too far north to be able to go down towards Australia. This thought kept me up at night. I couldn't stop thinking about a Dutch ocean rower who, just the year before, had also left from Peru for Australia and was pushed by these currents a few miles from the Galapagos. After a frightening shipwreck on the coral barrier of a Tonga cay, he'd escaped with his life, but he'd had to give up the adventure.

In those hectic days, Rick twice told us all that optimal weather conditions were coming and suggested we consider the possibility of leaving immediately. Regretfully, I had to say no, because even though we'd worked really hard, I hadn't yet finished painting the hull with antifouling paint, which was a long, difficult process. Francesca was also still busy loading the 650 pounds of food on board. She had loaded so much that the rations for the first two weeks had to be put in a waterproof bag under the sliding seat. On February 4, her mother had also arrived and offered her complete help.

Because of the constant delays and setbacks, I had stopped being able to contain my nerves, and at the slightest thing I would burst out in anger. Every morning, I read the weather forecast and stopped to study the direction of the clouds and tried to make forecasts. The wind was very strong on average. It often blew in a direction that, if I were at sea would have pushed me far to the north of the optimal course. If there's one phrase that could describe my mood in those days, it would be "overwhelming state of anxiety". I tried as best as I could to conceal it, especially from Francesca, but I don't think I much succeeded.

Allowing ourselves a short break in a small tourist town in the north of Peru helped us spend a bit of time quietly together before we got overwhelmed by events. But as soon as we got back from that short vacation, the departure was again a point of true agony. It had been four years since my first unsuccessful attempt to cross the Atlantic, interrupted just six hours after my departure in Genoa because of unfavorable conditions. My memory of it was still crystal clear. It would have definitely given me a bit of hope to see some sign of the weather conditions improving, but they weren't.

Actually, the more time passed, the less ready I felt to leave. This feeling weighed on me and made me feel a lot of tension, especially when I happened to catch Francesca's eyes and often saw her lost in thought and worried. One of the sweetest, saddest memories I have of that time on land was when I was helping her arrange the food in vacuum packs in the galley. I took out packs and passed one at a time to her as she crouched in the cabin. It was a long, boring job, but the atmosphere was cheerful and relaxed. But a little bit later, because of a little spat, I saw her crying, lying in her cabin with her hands over her face. It was then that I realized that we had more to lose than to gain in this adventure.

I'd learned to live with fear in that period. Shipwrecks, failure, and death were common worries, but I accepted them because I thought, rather fatalistically, they were unpredictable eventualities that were beyond my control. Unfortunately, it wasn't only up to us if the crossing would fail or succeed. There was unquestionably a greater likelihood it being interrupted midway than my getting to the other part of the Pacific, but I wanted at least to try. I was only sure of one thing: I wouldn't die. Whatever happened to me, I would come home. This little certainty gave me much comfort. At least a couple of times, the Atlantic Ocean had brought me very close to death, but since then I'd gained knowledge. I'd matured and those past experiences were a distant memory. But I had frequent nightmares and even hours after I woke, it took a long time for the feelings to fade. I often dreamed that I left, forgetting something essential on land, forcing me to abandon the adventure. This was one of the biggest fears.

On February 18, having studied his forecast models, Rick Shema identified a window of particularly favorable weather conditions for Sunday, the 21st. It was only three days away. From that moment on, time passed in a blur. We had managed to plan our final commitments to keep the last day all for ourselves. Sun, sea, some relaxation, and a big lunch. Who knows why, but of all the things I could want before leaving, the last dinner always had an almost sacred importance. For my last evening on land, I wanted to have a surprise for Francesca, but I was kept in bed by a high fever and nausea all of the next afternoon. So we just had dinner in a fast food restaurant, but I remember it as the most romantic dinner of my life.

Early the next morning, there was one last formality to take care of: getting the exit stamp on my passport. For this last task, our friend Renzo went with us. As was often the case here, what happened made us feel like we were on Candid Camera. The area where the offices were located, not far from the Port of Callao, was not a safe area for foreigners. There were often muggings on taxis of tourists who were robbed of everything they had on them. Plus, only a few daring taxi drivers agreed to take fares to these areas. We had parked the Renzo's car right in front of the entrance to the building to minimize the risk of being attacked. We were accompanied to the passport control office by an armed guard. As soon as we got into the building, we heard the rapid steps of an elderly woman who shook her hands heavenward like she wanted to invoke the grace of God. She ran towards us, saying, "Sir, sir. Your car. It's been taken!" All we needed was to have our car stolen! We all ran to the exit, looking at each other quizzically. In the place where the car had been a few seconds earlier, we found a small sticker on the sidewalk. The sticker said that the car had been towed by the police and the owner could go to a nearby garage to claim it. Renzo just had to go to the garage and show his driver's license to a policeman with fifty dollars in it, and he got his car back. On this trip, Peru had shown us its worst face, that of corruption. From that moment on, I was overcome the profound desire to put as much ocean as possible between me and that country, which from the day we arrived had done nothing but give us unpleasant surprises.

When we got to the boating club, I found a huge number of people crowded on the wharf. They were all staring at my rowboat moored a few dozen yards away. At that moment, I was already gone. Anyone who looked me straight in the eye would have seen only distance. I felt very far away from all that hubbub, as if I were already enveloped in the peace of my first day at sea. Those last moments on land, I was in a bit of a haze. Everything I did or said, the only detail of which I was conscious was Francesca's hand squeezing mine.

Though when I woke up that morning, the weather conditions had been perfect, the sky at noon was completely clouded over. The wind came up in gusts every so often strong enough to pull the beach umbrellas out of the sand. Grudgingly, I decided up until the last minute not to exclude the possibility of putting off my departure. Only if the weather gave me total assurance, would I go. The worst mistake I could make would be to be influenced by the many people crowding around me who came only to see me leave.

I remember one day when an old sailor from Genoa had told me that the skill of a good sailor isn't knowing how to weather the worst conditions, but it's knowing not to leave if the conditions aren't right. I hadn't finished the thought when I was already on my boat to untie the knot that kept it attached to a buoy. I looked around and saw a quiet crowd watching me, awaiting a signal or movement from me. I waited to feel the tension in my muscles that was the clear sign that the moment to leave had come. I hesitated a few seconds, then I sat on the seat, took the oars in my hands and said to myself: OK, let's go. A second later, the Club de Regattas' siren sounded to signal my first strokes towards the open ocean.

For about thirty minutes I was followed by a small boat holding Francesca, her mother, and some Club members. They stayed at a distance so I couldn't talk to them without shouting. There wasn't much to say anyhow. At a certain point, I stopped and let their boat get close and signaled that they should go back. We were about a mile and half from the shore and it was time for them to go back. I kissed Francesca for the last time and started rowing. In those seconds when I took my course westwards and she towards land, I felt like I could feel in the air between her and me all of the solitude and sadness that we would go through, alone, until I got to Australia. It wasn't long before her figure was lost on the horizon. In the two hundred ninety-four days that followed, other than my breath and the wind, the noise of my thoughts, the creaking of the boat, and every now and then a roar of thunder, I would hear almost no other sound.

Land, February 2008

I was tense the day of his departure. I hadn't slept a wink the night before. There were so many people at the Club de Regattas and so much hustle and bustle, but we were in such a state of bewilderment that we hardly noticed. You could tell a mile away that, mentally, Alex was already gone.

When he pushed off from the dock, I followed him on a motorboat for a few miles. While on land, he seemed impatient, but with those first oar strokes he became visibly calmer. It was like putting a fish back in water. He rowed quickly and his movements gave no sign of the effort it must have taken to move that boat weighing over a ton. He seemed to glide over the water. I think that those first oar strokes contained all his impatience for something so long desired. Now he was free to go and get what he wanted, he'd said to me, almost like he was leaving for a trip just out of town.

The motorboat stayed by him for more than a half hour. I could have whispered something to him, but I hadn't managed to say anything when he suddenly stopped, stood up from the seat and asked me to turn back. He leaned over the edge of his boat and gave me a kiss, "We'll talk later… "

In a second, he was gone past the horizon and then everything went back to regular life.

I got a call from Alex after a few hours. I hadn't expected him to call so soon. When he heard my voice, he burst into tears. They were tears full of the tension he hadn't managed to release before; it was a moment of true suffering. I hoped he would quickly be able to get used to his new situation. I hoped that the lights of Lima would disappear quickly from the horizon because only then would he be able to separate himself from what tied him to the land. In those early days, my mother often asked me how I was doing. I asked her to wait a while to ask me. I felt good, strong, full of energy, and calm, though I was afraid I might break down suddenly. I returned to Italy the next week. At home, our dog Dusty was overjoyed to see me, but he was disappointed to see me alone.

I was really happy to be back in Trieste. I didn't know what it would be like going back to our house, now empty and without all the things that had filled it and were now on board the *Rosa d'Atacama II.*

I put the keys on the table and realized that there was a note under the fruit bowl. I picked it up and immediately recognized Alex's handwriting. I recalled the moment in the night in which we left Italy when Alex had closed himself in the kitchen. I had heard him rip a piece of paper from his notebook. At the time, I hadn't thought about what he was doing.

"Welcome home."

The feeling that that piece of paper gave me was a sweet as his caress. In the following days, I found many others. More than thirty. In the bathroom cabinet, in the saltshaker in the kitchen, under the pillow, in the silverware drawer, and even between the towels. They were everywhere. But I didn't want to read them all right away. I wanted the surprise to last. So I decided to read them bit-by-bit, anytime I wanted to feel like he was with me. Another example of how present Alex was in my life was on my birthday, December 17, when he had me find his birthday message written on our bedroom ceiling with a red spray can. That was Alex: fun and unpredictable.

Leaving behind the world of shadows, February 21, 2008

I left land with a sea breeze from southeast. An excellent eastern current helped me move away from land at a decent speed. The last image I had of land was of enormous waves violently crashing against the cliffs on the southern tip of the gulf where the Club de Regattas was located. The sea was so full and smashed into the rocks with such violence that I was afraid for a moment that once night came, that dark, shadowy mass would swallow me up. The feeling stayed with me that night and for many nights to come.

My boat was so heavily loaded with food and equipment that nothing more could have fit. It had been a real challenge to get it all in and I'd given up bringing some books in the end. It heaved on the water like on old truck on a bumpy country road, but I was so full of energy that I got it up to a good speed right away. The waterline was submerged by about two inches fore to aft. Water poured into the openings on the freeboard made to let water drain out if the deck flooded. In those early days, I had to apply so much force to the oars to keep it in motion that the ligaments in my wrists and shoulders ached at night. As evening approached, the breeze died down and the sea became calm and as smooth as oil. I stopped to rest for an hour and cooked some freeze-dried pasta. I soaked up the pleasure of having regained my connection to the sea in that surreal peace. I'd forgotten how beautiful it was. When I close my eyes I can still feel those first moments of solitude, the simultaneous emptiness and fullness. There was the feeling of exhaustion merged with that of energy and agitation. It was in that brief moment that I was struck full force by the boundless adventure I had undertaken. It would be hundreds of days, thousands of hours, millions of oar strokes before I would reach any land on other side of the Pacific. Who could say if that time would be enough to help me understand who I really am? The immensity of the ocean was before me, but that first evening I often looked back, searching the land. I was curious to see if even a tiny piece of it was left, as if I were seeking a final contact with it. I already missed Francesca terribly.

The first days went by quickly and without problem. But it must have been at least ten days before I managed to get into a daily routine. It was a slow process to get the hang of the rhythms and habits of the sea. The long hours at the oars, the early morning alarm, the food and physical pains, calluses, blisters on my backside, and sunburns. Before the end of the second week, I felt much more relaxed and in tune with my new situation. The sky was still cloudy and I hadn't much worried about putting on strong sunscreen. This was a huge mistake because I was immediately badly burned on my thighs and neck. I put a piece fabric on the back of my hat to cover my shoulders and I wrapped by burnt legs with two sheet pieces.

Though I was progressing at a good pace, psychologically I went through a few difficult days. I was melancholy. I felt like my heart was being squeezed in a vice. Francesca and I talked often, at least a couple of times a day. I tried to explain to her what was forcing me into this state of mind.

The problem of the blisters on my backside worsened so much in the following weeks that for two days I had been unable to row. I found temporary relief by covering the irritated area with Vaseline. I made a try at rowing naked, but the greasy layer both didn't let my skin breathe and made me rather slippery on the seat. At the worst moments, I'd even had to take some painkillers. It was excruciating, like having little needles stuck in my skin every time I moved on the seat. The problem cleared up after a few days and I went back to rowing, but occasionally the pain reared its head again.

These were the days of my first encounters with a strange jellyfish called Portuguese man-o-war. On March 27, after only thirty-six days at sea, I noted in my logbook that many barnacles had started to populate the underwater part of the hull. These living creatures are crustaceans and have soft bodies and hard tips like a small mussel. They can grow up to two inches long. They can attach themselves to any surface, including the hull of boats, slowing them a great deal as they did to mine. This was an unhappy surprise after everything I had done to avoid the problem. I was forced to solve it the same way I had dozens of times when crossing the Atlantic. I had to dive underwater to clean it off with a plastic spatula. Though it wasn't a dangerous thing to do, I did have to consider certain risks. As I had to put my head underwater I could be hit by the boat and a blow to the head could knock me out. But this wasn't the only risk.

Though I'd thought that marine animals, particularly sharks, could be a major danger, I had completely underestimated jellyfish. The first calm day at sea, I had gone in the water and tried to get the barnacles off of the hull. I had almost finished when I felt a stinging sensation on my left thigh, like a burn that quickly spread to my whole leg. At first I thought that a big fish had bitten me and I had to look at my leg to make sure it was still attached. I jumped back on the boat as quickly as possible. After I rinsed off at length, trying to get off some of the little tentacles left attached to my leg, I spread on a cortisone cream. A bit later I was feeling better and the burning was limited only to where I had the sting. About a half hour later, when I started rowing again, I saw it right in front of me! It was a Portuguese man-o-war, a common name for *physalia physalis*, a jellyfish typical of tropical seas. They aren't true jellyfish, but a colony of small polyps with intensely stinging tentacles. It had long electric blue tentacles, which were still stuck to the right oar's shaft and the air sac that made it float was hanging in the air. That was my first encounter with the Australian jellyfish, and it wouldn't be the last. In the future, I would have to be more careful and keep my eyes wide open. On my course, I often met another kind of jellyfish, called *velella velella* or "Jack-sail-by-the-wind". They are small, flat, circular organisms, a few inches across that have a small veil that lets them move by wind power. They have quite short tentacles, which means you are less likely to be stung by them, but they are so lightweight that the water quite often picks them up and carries them for hundreds of yards through the air.

My first encounter with this little creature happened on a very windy day while I was cooking in the cabin. The door was open, as I usually left it when I was cooking, and I was concentrated on the gas burner and the pan of boiling water. All of the sudden I felt a sharp sting on one knee, which made me jump back. I thought I'd been burned by the burner, but it was a little velella that had been picked up by the wind and ended up in my cabin. But the stinging was much less severe than it had been from the Portuguese man-o-war. There was no peace to be had with those little jellyfish everywhere. Not even in my own cabin! But definitely the funniest, most unexpected thing happened a few months later when I got in the water to wash off. I usually washed when it was only absolutely necessary, which is when the salt water on my skin became unbearable and I wanted to get rid of the layers of sunscreen, or just when my body really needed it. Sometimes the smell coming off of me was terrible. At sea, far from everyone, you lose all your inhibitions. Even though these quick baths had a good effect on my muscles and on my mood alike, they were a hassle because at the end of the day I was always tired and I just wanted to eat and get into my sleeping bag as quickly as possible. Sometimes rather than jumping into the ocean, I would just pour a bucket of seawater over my head and rub a sponge energetically over my creased skin. It was a much faster method and I preferred it because I didn't like to get in water at night. On that day, the sea was unusually calm and on my lunch break I took the chance for a quick swim, I got in the water and a velella stung me on my genitals. It was a terrible sensation, like having a mousetrap clamped between your legs. The pain left me breathless for a few seconds, though, thankfully, it didn't last long.

Land, March 2008

At home I worked on the project a lot and I was relaxed. I knew that Alex was doing well at sea and was starting slowly to get used to his new lifestyle. I soon realized that he depended on me and my moods a lot. If when we talked by satellite phone, if I was happy and calm, it all went well for him. Whereas if he heard even a hint of tiredness in my voice, he got gloomy and tense. For him, the separation was harder than he'd imagined. I knew he was overcome by moments of great homesickness. He said he felt powerless because he'd wanted to stay by my side, but he couldn't hide from himself his desire to go. He was true to himself, even though it was very hard. But, though it'd been very difficult to leave land, he had plenty of motivation to go on. He knew that to see me again all he could do was row!

We talked regularly, two or three times a day, and we'd plan a time for the next call. With the alternation of different time zones, it was never daytime for us at the same time. The morning call was always my favorite. Alex told me how his day had gone. He was relaxed and getting ready for bed, after having written in his logbook, which was published on his web site. He had taken it on as a commitment, feeling it as a duty to the thousands of people who followed him online. He didn't want to disappoint the expectations of those at home who followed his every move in the middle of the ocean. He often told me that they helped him find the strength to continue when he was exhausted. There were a lot of people who had hopes and dreams for adventure stored aboard that boat. Looking at anyone's life I could see a small or large ocean that they had to cross; whether it was in their work, love lives, or family lives, everyone had a challenge to face. This helped me once again see Alex's experience as totally normal. I never managed to think of it as something extraordinary, but simply how he lived his life.

Once he said to me that he would not want to get to middle age, having traveled the earth and explored its remotest corners, if he didn't have someone by him to share it with; without someone by his side and children to tell about it. It was then that I took Alex off of the pedestal I'd put him on years earlier.

This is another reason why I feel lucky to have a man like him by my side, a man whose main goal is to be himself to be able to be with me in peace. This is why I have always tried to support Alex in his choices. No matter what people might assume, I never felt alone, not even one day, during his entire crossing of the Pacific.

S 10° 34' – W 96° 38', March 2008

For the first month, the weather conditions were pretty good and I was able to cover a good distance. At the pace of my new routine, days became weeks, then months went by. Time started to lose its identity; it no longer had a name, just a number in a row. The sea under me slipped by with the same maddening slowness as the clouds that quietly glided westwards. Sometimes great cloud masses cloaked the sky and sea in black. They would often dump huge amounts of water, but then after a few hours, the sun shone again and the heat went back to baking my skin. I soon learned to appreciate and make use of these events that could be incredibly intense. I used any object that could hold water, the pan for heating up my food and water bottles, to gather small amounts of rain to use for cooking and brushing my teeth. It tasted a bit salty, but it wasn't too annoying. The rainwater was very useful for another reason. It let me rinse my clothes and wash the saltwater off of my skin. Particularly under my armpits, between my legs and in all of my body's folds where it made my skin itchy and irritated. Including the water I drank and that I used to cook, I used about two and a half gallons of water a day. It took me three hours every evening to desalinate that amount with my manual device. So every single drop of rain I collected meant a great deal to me. I always tried to avoid wasting it. I had slowly gotten used to drinking less of it than I needed. The desalinator was a device like a tube with a steel arm on the end that served as a pump. By inverse osmosis, the water was pumped within a very thin membrane and the difference in pressure made the salt stay inside the membrane and be automatically expelled with a tube. Working this mechanism was always really tiring. So there were many days in which, instead of desalinating the water by hand, I attached the pump with its steel arm to my sliding seat. This let me desalinate some water using a lot less energy. The water that it made was pure and clean, without the slightest taste of salt. I wouldn't have been able to tell the difference from bottled mineral water. The only nuisance was that I drank only room-temperature water. On those days when I was rowing through very warm waters, up to 75 degrees F, it was a bit disgusting. I can't tell you what I would have given for a cool drink. On particularly warm days, when the afternoon sun beat hard, my need to drink skyrocketed and two and a half gallons was often not enough. I looked around me at all the salt water that slid under my keel greedy to make it mine. It was cruel that I couldn't just bend down and drink it all.

I focused my rowing in the hours between dawn and dusk. However, not infrequently, when conditions were particularly favorable, I kept on rowing late into the night. Though in the evening, it was great to be able to row without the sun's oppressive heat, the tiredness that built up over long night hours did not always justify the small distance I covered. You had to have a huge amount of tolerance for frustration to make it through a night of rowing. The hours always passed excruciatingly slowly and monotonously. Fighting off sleepiness could be a major challenge. Yet, these moments were also full of powerful emotions too. The dark of the night made me feel closer to the sky and the darkness opened my eyes to unknown worlds whose existence was hidden from me in the light of the day. The water shone with minuscule life forms. Sudden flashes like lightening in the sky lit up its depth. At those moments I thought how I actually knew only a tiny sliver of the sea despite the many weeks I had spent in close contact with it. What was hiding under the water's surface was a mystery as fascinating to me as what the heavens hold.

I had gotten in the habit of waking up at five thirty in the morning, in the semi-darkness. As soon as the sun rose, the cabin quickly became very hot and the air was unbreathable. I'd have a big breakfast with muesli and powdered milk, some cookies or rice cakes with jam. I often ended up eating a few small, flying fish that fell into the boat in the night. With the first light of morning, I sat down and started where I had left off the night before. The sea never ceased to amaze me. It was a chameleon that changed its appearance with the sun's reflections. The dawn's light tinged it a purplish red. As the ball of fire rose in the sky, it gradually took on silver streaks on its surface, like millions of tiny pieces of glass that dazzled my eyes. At midday, the sea seemed something else entirely. The sun rays came as straight as punches, flashing turquoise light so brilliant that it seemed as if you could see to the very bottom. As the hours passed and night drew close, it returned to its silvery color and then fiery red. The sea kept on surprising me even at night. Oddly enough, it seemed to come to life when the sun went down.

Every morning, it was very hard to start rowing again. The repetitiveness of the days, the accumulated fatigue and muscle pain were so great that there were days when I didn't want to ever get out of bed. Sometimes I was in such a bad mood that a mere little physical ache could make me stay in the cabin the whole day and do crossword puzzles. On those days, I slept a lot, making up for the hours of sleep I'd lost, but when I woke up, I was always in a pool of sweat and an even worse mood because I felt stupid, ridiculous and really guilty for not having rowed. Francesca could always tell my mood from my tone of voice. She would always say that a little rest could only do me good.

"You're not in a race against time. Don't forget that. Enjoy the trip and be happy every day because soon it will just be a memory."

Unfortunately, I often forgot how exceptional my experience was, not being just an athletic endeavor, but one of personal growth. If I'd always kept this fact in mind, maybe I wouldn't have settled for watching days go by in front of my cabin window, and I would have made more effort to experience it more intensely.

The monotony of my days, each so much like the next, was broken up by short breaks to eat and drink, and a longer break from one to two in the afternoon for lunch. My lunch usually left me not completely satisfied. The amount of food I ate was designed to meet my caloric needs, but it didn't feel like enough to me. To feel fuller, I ate slowly, chewing each mouthful for a long time. When I could, I added a small amount of dry or raw fish. On the days that the blisters on my backside caused unbearable pain, I spent my hour-long break standing outside of the cabin, holding my little pot. There were some days that were different because the sea and wind were so rough that it was dangerous to be outside of the cabin. I could only spend my time in my wet, cramped space. This didn't usually happen for more than three or four days in a row, but sometimes bad conditions could go on for ten long days. At twenty knots, the wind raised 9-feet high waves. The boat lurched and became unmanageable. With the oars alone, there was no way for me to control it. Then there was nothing I could do but throw in one of the three floating anchors that I had to slow the speed of the boat and stabilize it. It drove me crazy having to be stuck in the cabin, without moving. It was my only shelter, but it was too small to get comfortable. I wrote a lot on those days, filling pages and pages of my logbook with closely-packed handwriting, verging on manic. Word after word, I started to notice the therapeutic effect of hours spent with pen in hand. Rowing made me face myself and writing made me lay myself bare. When I wasn't writing, I was reading. I was a voracious reader and after about two months I had read more than half of the books I had loaded on board. I had books of every kind and for every taste, from police stories to crime thrillers and, of course, biographies of adventurers and stories of adventure, and even the philosophical and humanistic writings of Schopenhauer. The story of the survivors of an airplane crash in the Andes in the 1970s made a big impression on me. It was a story that was known around the world. Though I'd already heard about it, it was only in reading it that I really understood the full horror, desperation and desire to live of those involved. I was so struck by the book that when I finished reading it, I decided to fast for twenty-four hours in honor of the sacrifices made by those young people to survive the disaster that had befallen them.

With the few things I had on board and some imagination, I tried to find good alternatives to reading and writing. One day, for fun, I took some of the empty packages of freeze-dried food, folded them, cut them and decorated them to create some small flowers like daisies, Francesca's favorite flower. They would be the first flowers I'd give her when we saw each other again. I even liked to carve the little pieces of wood that I had taken on board if I needed them to make a repair. With a sharp knife I made abstract forms, then honed them with sandpaper to make them smooth as glass. Though the results weren't always great, it was a perfect way to relax. Solitude was something I had sought out and really wanted. Without this aspect of isolation from the rest of the world, I might not have taken on a trip like this. Recalling my crossing of the Atlantic, I could really get the essence of this new trip only if I could do it alone. The solitude combined with the vastness of the sea, beyond any conceivable limit and without visual reference points had laid the foundation for the most exceptional adventure I could have. My adventure, day after day, little by little, was losing its meaning as a trip towards a geographic destination. It was taking on a new meaning, that of an introspective experience, a trip into the weaknesses and darkness of a person on a quest towards a greater knowledge and awareness of himself. Reaching Australia was still the goal I was after, but in all those days spent isolated at sea, between the starry sky and the wild sea, I had fully understood that the true meaning of travel is the trip itself, wherever it takes you.

On this adventure across the Pacific, I couldn't but marvel at the clear contradictions and contrasts all around me. There was the immensity of the sea in extreme contrast with the tight space of my little boat. There was the sense of independence that I got from doing what I'd most wanted that came through a world of sacrifices. At the times that the elements turned against me, showing me their frightening side, I felt small and fragile at the same time as a deep sense of freedom, harmony, and belonging to nature.

My isolation also contrasted with my actual ability to communicate. I was only seemingly alone. Being of the multi-media, high-tech generation, I could make use of satellite communication tools that let me keep in contact with my support team and the thousands of people who followed me on the Internet.

Friday was the day I connected to the microphones of Caterpillar, an Italian radio show on Radio2. Opening the phone call was a fragment of a song by an Italian singer, Mirco Menna, called “L’arcobaleniere” (meaning, roughly, “rainbow man”). I was always thrilled to hear it because talking on the radio was fun and it marked the time, reminding me that another week had passed. I told the two hosts, Massimo Cirri and Filippo Solibello, and all their listeners about my adventure and opened a view of a world that looked surreal from land. Those few minutes a week were like a breath of fresh air for me. Spurred by the two hosts’ sense of humor, I tried to bring out the most fun, entertaining aspects of the experience. It wasn’t easy. There were times I just wanted to scream and whine, but I always tried to keep a cheerful tone. The warmth and encouragement of all those people was really amazing. Though I didn’t know any of them personally, I’d grown fond of them. I made some good friendships and soon it was like we’d known each other forever.

The satellite positioning system, “GPS”, almost completely erased the chance of getting lost at sea. The safety systems with which I was equipped would let me send an SOS in dangerous situations. I thought a lot about the conditions in which seafarers had lived up until fifty years ago. Once they left, there was no trace of them and nothing was known until they came back. All these modern devices that we can use today mean greater safety so that we can sometimes dare more than would have been possible in the past. Adventure back then had a completely different taste.

Land, summer 2008

Alex was subject to frequent mood swings. Sometimes, he would admit how tired he was from rowing and say he really wanted to take a day off, but he was afraid to do it to disappoint his and my expectations. He's always had a deep sense of duty. At those times, I tried to tell him why he should allow time for himself and the journey he had undertaken. I tried to remind him that it wasn't just a chance to cross the ocean for him. These were moments that would soon be only a memory. It seemed important to me that he give himself the luxury of bringing home with him the colors and smells of a few lazy days off too.

When Alex was in the middle of the sea, I was often invited to take part in events during which we made a satellite connection. It was exciting to think how we could be in a conference room and in just a few seconds reach him and hear his voice. He seemed much closer than he was. Technology really overcame and erased distance. Sometimes, in front of people, I would get emotional hearing him speak. Maybe it was only then that I really understood what he was doing. He had found the courage to take charge of his life and look for what was his. This always struck me as truly magnificent. I'd often heard Alex say to an audience that anyone could row across an ocean if that person really wanted it. This was a big statement that could make people laugh or misunderstand, but Alex showed me that nothing is truer.

There are no impossible goals as long as there are no limits in our minds. When we deeply believe in what we're doing and that we can realize our plan, then everything becomes easy. Almost like magic, we find everything falling into place. It isn't just chance. We are the ones who make it happen, if we are ready to change and accept redefining and reconsidering our goals with new criteria based on making them happen. Muscles, physical training, and natural talent; there had to be something more than just a desire. Alex told how during his previous crossing of the Atlantic, starting on the second day, he started to row with his mind rather than the muscles of his arms.

S 11° 10′ – W 88° 38′, March 2008

One evening, just before going to bed, I realized that many dorados were swimming around my boat. Dorados are commonly known as dolphin fish. I had seen them and caught a lot of them both in the Mediterranean and the Atlantic. Until then, I hadn't seen fish so close up. I couldn't wait to catch one to add it to my diet. The dark seemed to calm them, as they swam around me like they were in a deep sleep. With my head lamp I could light only a small part of the sea. I clearly saw the outline of their figures moving beneath me. The darkness gave me the best chance to surprise them and my best hope of getting one with my spearfishing rifle.

Dorados are beautiful fish, great fighters, and wily predators. Their favorite prey is flying fish. If you've never seen a flying fish, you would be amazed by this particular cross between a marine animal and a bird. I remember when I saw it for the first time, I could hardly believe my eyes. When it is chased, it tries to throw off its pursuer by jumping out of the water and gliding quickly and far. The dorados, considering this ability of their favorite prey, have adapted their hunting techniques. I often saw them on long chases, leaping quickly out of water to not let their prey get away. They are decked out in very dazzling colors, from green to bright blue. In the water, the effect of the sun makes them even seem golden. They have an exceptional quality that I've never seen in other fish. Right before they die, they temporarily lose their flashy coloring, fading to a pale gray. Then, just a few seconds later, they get it back. They can easily grow up to six feet long and weigh over 45 pounds. The one I caught that night was no more than 11 pounds, but I was very happy anyway. The spearfishing rifle worked great, but I could have used more practice. I shot and missed about twenty times before I got one. The dolphin fish weren't the only ones I managed to catch on my crossing. I caught some beautiful skipjacks, in the tuna family, and some small mackerel. I liked to eat them raw to keep their nutritional value intact, adding soy sauce or olive oil, but I also really enjoyed the fish dried in the sun or marinated in lemon juice. With no way of storing it in a cool place, I had to eat it within thirty six hours. Once I did eat some more than three days after it was caught. This was a big mistake. I paid for it with awful intestinal problems. From that day on, I made the strict rule that I had to throw into the sea all the fish I couldn't finish.

The flying fish were also an excellent food source, and it hardly took any effort to catch them. None too rarely, in the morning I would gather some of decent size right outside of my cabin. After cleaning them, I cooked them in the pan with some seawater. One night when I was sleeping, a flying fish came into my cabin through a small window that I had left open to let in air. It had slipped in at just the right angle to fly into my sleeping bag.

Feeding myself with what the sea had to offer made me feel like I was an essential part of the sea, in its natural cycle, like all of the other marine creatures. I'd gotten in the habit of throwing a fishing line and lure in the water every morning. Usually I had enough luck that I would find a fish on the hook before evening. But I'd noticed that the fishing was better in the first ten days of the lunar cycle. After that, the line could be in the water for days and days without getting anything. In the evening, before sundown was the best time for fishing. The water would be teeming with fish, mainly tuna, flipping and flopping like lunatics under my boat. They often banged into the hull. All I had to do was shoot in the midst of them and there was a good chance of hitting one of them. In late March, I noticed a small clear mark on one of the two flexible solar panels installed on the cabin. I hadn't noticed it right away. I wrote it in my logbook with a big question mark next to it. Not knowing what to do, I decided to keep an eye on it. A few days later, I mentioned it to Roger, who was in charge of both meteorological monitoring and the technical aspects of the onboard electronic instruments. On the power meter installed in the cabin, I hadn't noticed any obvious changes in the amount of energy supplied by the solar panels. Roger suggested I immediately run a check on each individual panel.

The two electric panels that managed the power were in the fore cabin for that purpose, which was also used for storing food and equipment. The first day of calm sea, I made room between the watertight bags that filled the cabin. I crawled in with a power meter. Two of the seven solar panels, all from the same manufacturer, showed a drastic decline in the electric supply! I was really shaken up by the discovery. I had to sit down in the cabin for a few minutes to come to grips with it. If that problem spread to the rest of the solar panels, it could have meant giving up the entire crossing because without the electronic equipment on board, especially the GPS and radar, it would be suicidal to go through the thousands of coral islands that would soon be in my path. For the entire day and night, I hadn't been able to stave off a horrible sense of failure. I imagined myself forced to stop the crossing, turning back to the closest coast. The next morning I woke up sure that it would be my last day at sea.

A few days went by, and, though my mood was still low, I started to think that it would be possible to survive this new situation. In fact, I'd been doing just fine and had started to think of the unexpected event as a new challenge to overcome. In reality, the reduced energy available had had no consequences, as the remaining panels had been enough to cover my main needs. After that, I learned the importance of managing my stress, fear, and worries. It took weeks, but I'd learned to live with that strange feeling of unease caused by the imponderable uncertainty of life at sea. In the past, in the Atlantic, it had so strongly affected me that it contributed a lot to the food on board running out ahead of schedule. As for fear, I had started to see it as a right. Later, in the most extreme situations, I wouldn't be afraid of fear. In fact, I had learned to understand the courage of fear, the kind of headlong, desperate daring that could come instinctively out of a dangerous situation. It might seem strange, but for me fear has always been a comforting companion. At any rate, where there's fear, there's awareness.

One day, after only seventy-two days, I had just finished lunch and sat down on the sliding seat to start rowing again. It was really hot. The sea was calm and not even the sound of wind could be heard. I needed to desalinate some water again because I had drunk a lot that day, so I connected the desalinating device to the sliding seat. As soon as I moved my legs I heard a sound like a plastic bottle crumpling. I couldn't tell exactly what the sound was right away. Turning around I saw the watermaker, the same one that had been with me for the entire Atlantic crossing, without ever giving a sign of fatigue, broken in two. Maybe I had moved my legs too brusquely or maybe the piston had suddenly locked. Whatever the reason, the pump was broken in two clean parts. I stood up and took a step back, shaking my head disbelievingly. From further away, it looked even sorrier. For the second time in just over two weeks, I sat in my cabin with my hands in my hair, sure that this was it for my time at sea. Before I left, Francesca had absolutely insisted that I bring two water desalinators, so I'd bought another one as a back up, which had proved a lifesaver. Because of a lack of room on board, I hadn't been able to load even a small supply of drinking water. Now that I considered it, that had been quite a risk, but I had so much faith in my two watermakers that I had felt safe. The new device became the only source of drinking water left, except for the rain. That evening I prayed for a long time before sleeping. In this desperation, I felt alone for the first time.

From then on, I used the water desalinator with meticulous care. For a few weeks, I continued to use it as I had before, connected to the seat, but as soon as I started to hear the first suspicious sounds, I took it off and started to use it by hand. Every time I used it, I talked to it, begging it to keep going until we got to land. At the end of the day I put it in a dry corner, optimistic that it would get to Australia before it broke, but I have to say my hands shook every time I used it. Technically, these two unexpected events, first the solar panels and then the desalinator, hadn't caused obvious damage yet and maybe with a little care, they never would. But my own negative, self-defeating thoughts were what caused my only real problems. They had affected my morale so much that all I had to do was imagine colliding with a ship and I'd spend the whole night with my ears straining for any noise. Yet, likewise, if I just imagined coming into the bay of Sydney, I'd get excited and row until late at night. I had to work on my thinking, force myself to keep a positive attitude, if I wanted things to keep on going well.

Honestly, it was harder than I'd ever imagined. In times of weakness, particular frustration, I took out all of my stress and disappointment on food. I stuffed myself until I couldn't get anymore in. But after the first rush of pleasure, I would be overwhelmed by a sense of guilt.

This happened quite regularly. Aware of the harm I was doing myself, I set "fasts". For varying lengths of time, to clean my conscience, I gave up eating something tasty. I'd done it with chocolate, with cookies, and with nougat, but as I was able to set myself a strict regime and respect the fast to the letter, as soon as the time was up, not a minute later, I rewarded myself by gorging on chocolate, with the excuse that I'd been good, and the whole cycle started again.

As the months passed and the days became slower and more monotonous, only every now and then something happened worth telling about in my logbook. Pages that said "uneventful day" were very many. I started to feel a bit disappointed.

The southeast trade winds had been with me for many months until I reached the first French Polynesian islands, the Marquesas and Tuamotu. Some days, the wind blew impetuously like a flooding river. The ocean would rise up over ten feet. Other times, the water was so calm and smooth that I could stand on one leg and keep my balance.

On nights like that, the moon reflected on the motionless sea. The two images, the real and reflected one, became one. It was so immense, silent, and uninhabited that I felt as light as a feather. Those evenings were the best for stargazing. With the help of a stargazing manual, I learned the names and locations of many constellations that filled much of the southern hemisphere. Every so often, I used their position to keep on course.

I saw so many birds! Some species were tireless migratory birds that went thousands of miles from land, but usually the smaller species meant land wasn't far off. Each bird had its style of flight and its hunting habits. Silly swimmers or skilled divers, solitary or grouped in large colonies, I grew very attached to their company. There were two different species of booby birds, a large bird common in the Galapagos Islands. They were the funniest birds I'd ever come across. A *masked booby*, so called for its black coloring around its eyes that looks like a mask, got close to me on a day when the sea was very rough. He seemed to be looking for a safe place to rest and he stayed perched on my fore cabin for almost a week. During the day, he would go around my boat. Sometimes he got far enough away that I lost sight of him, but in the late afternoon, he returned to his place, on the cabin until the next morning. When I caught flying fish that were big enough, I tried to leave him a little piece, but he never accepted my gifts. He had a gentle, docile nature, more than many pets, and he never seemed afraid of me. In fact, I could get quite close to take some pictures. It moved me when sudden waves made him lose his balance and he fell in the water. It made me want to scoop him up and make room for him in the cabin.

A while later, he was joined by another species, a *blue-footed booby*, which was also common in the Galapagos Islands. He was so stubborn that it verged on the absurd. He had tried to get a grasp of the boat's side rails dozens of times without ever succeeding. Then he opted for the cabin, then the navigation lamp support, until he was worn out and he chose to perch on my head. Right on my head! His little talons stuck into my hat's canvas and scratched my scalp, giving me the chills. We were quite an odd couple, like a caricature. With his heedless, bold act, we cemented a relationship of brotherhood, as there is between all living beings.

I felt the same strong feeling of common belonging with the humpback and fin whales I came across. The thing that impressed me most wasn't the presence of animals that were so large and powerful that they could have split my little boat in two (consider that an adult blue whale can be up to 82-feet long and weigh over a hundred tons), but the wonder of seeing them emerge just a few feet from me, looking like a living creature from another planet. The more I looked at them the more I felt like I was looking at living fossils, primitive animals, mammals that learned how to adapt to aquatic life. I have to admit that sometimes they terrified me. One morning for almost two hours I was surrounded by four blue whales. I was very familiar with the story of Ambrogio Fogar and his seventy days drifting on a life raft, though in his case it was a killer whale that rammed and sunk his sailing boat. Out of fear of meeting his same fate, I didn't put my oars in the water to try to scatter them. The most amazing thing was the mighty blows they made to breathe. They had swum so close to me that a few times I'd even held my breath in fear.

Land, June 2008

In the months in which we planned the Pacific project, we never failed to talk about what to do if we had to handle an emergency. There was a big question on this point. If I hadn't heard from Alex by phone for a certain amount of time, how would I be able to tell if his boat moving on the water was pushed by currents or the power of his arms? If I couldn't get a hold of him by phone, how many hours should I wait before notifying an emergency rescue?

These were not easy conversations. Out of fear of jinxing it, Alex refused to even consider it.

I knew that some phone dates, even if set, could be skipped. Sometimes he might fall asleep exhausted without touching a bite to eat after a hard day; or problems with the satellite coverage, particularly in bad weather, could stop him from getting a connection. At those times Alex tried at least to send me a text message to assure me that all was fine.

But on that day I couldn't get a hold of him before going to sleep and the next morning I hadn't got a call. So I tried to call him myself, but the phone kept on ringing with no answer.

I wasn't worried. I was sure that the situation was under control, but I couldn't explain why he didn't answer. I remember that I joked with friends, pretending to be a jealous woman and imagining what scandalous encounters he might have in that uninhabited sea. Finally, after more than twelve hours of silence, Alex answered my umpteenth phone call with a whisper. Suddenly, from the other end of the line, I heard a strange noise that sounded like a burst of water. He spoke quietly and from the tone of his voice I realized he was very serious, but I didn't immediately understand what was happening. "I've been surrounded by some huge whales for more than an hour. They keep on swimming around my boat. They are so close, that I could have touched their backs, and I'm starting to get scared. Maybe they were just curious, but, believe me, I'm not having fun." My blood turned to ice. I couldn't fully grasp the situation, but the tone of his voice showed his worry.

Alex's encounters with sea animals had always a held a strange fascination and mystery for me when he told me about them. I was very impressed by his encounters with sharks, which happened almost always on the days when he dove down to clean off the hull. Once I asked him why he had to dive on the same days that he had already seen a shark, and he answered, "If I don't jump in the water right away, I'd never find the courage to do it again." He'd said it so simply that I couldn't argue.

I never thought something really serious could happen to him. I didn't think of him as a suicidal crazy man, or even someone who didn't have an understanding of the value of his life. On the contrary, I always thought that he felt its value so strongly that he did everything he could to not waste a moment of it. I knew that he was not an irresponsible person and that his sense of responsibility was even greater now that there were two of us. This always helped me take his adventure with great peace of mind. There were people around me who couldn't believe I could be so calm. His was not a fight against nature. That would be lost in the first round. It wasn't even a fight against himself. It wasn't a fight, that was all. To use a word that Alex likes a lot, it was first and foremost self-exploration.

Alex is enormously skilled at merging with the environment where he lives. He can very naturally slip into that universal mechanism that moves all living beings: the instinct for survival. A boat that goes about two knots and follows the ocean's movement, its currents, with no motor, and making no sound, seems like the perfect way to be able to merge with a seemingly hostile environment. Ultimately, it creates a great feeling of gratitude to Mother Nature.

S 12° 25' – W 128° 07', June 2008

The sea has always fascinated me with its immutable character, rendering it eternal, a work of art that defies time. That water sliding under my boat's keel had likely caressed the bodies of ancient creatures like dinosaurs, survived furious cataclysms, reached the sandy banks of the tropics, and merged with the icy water of the poles. It has crossed every boundary of time and space. Like the student of a wise Zen master, day after day, I felt part of all this by simply looking at it. Elusive horizons, lines that can never be touched, ephemeral sensations. Going by sea can make you feel like you are going nowhere. You go so slowly that it feels as if the Earth's rotation is making the sea move under your boat. For me, traveling (outside myself or within) is the most exciting, romantic way to spend my time, and it is what I love most, after my wife.

The sea was so vast that I couldn't find words to describe it. The feelings it spawned in me strained to find a way to be told. I was dazzled by the beauty before me. I already wondered what adjectives could describe this to those still on land, for whom I was the sole witness.

It is in our human nature to find it difficult to be in places as seemingly infinite as the sea. We need points of reference, directions, to orient ourselves in its vastness. As human beings facing the infinite, we suffer the fear of losing control over what happens. We no longer feel like we belong to anything. This is the true drama of pushing beyond your limits. Many times in Lima before I left, I stopped to look at the ocean. I could see thousands of square miles of it and then I imagined many more hidden beyond the horizon. My eyes were bewitched. I was drawn in, but I also felt a serious warning coming up from the depths of my soul. It was as if I heard a voice saying, "Be careful. Don't risk it. It's dangerous. The sea will swallow you." At that moment, my mind created frightening images of shipwrecks and storms, waves so high that I disappeared within them. It was a crazy man's idea. Who or what made me think I could take on this new challenge? In this state of inner debate, the infinite was intolerable for me too.

Between the fiery romanticism of the sunset and the dark mysticism of the night, there were always those times of day when life around me expressed its deepest meaning. When the day came to an end, the sky took on more dramatic colors, from yellow to indigo. Every evening, as the sun went down, mystery arose once again around that little boat of mine. One by one, the stars lit up like city lights. The night rose gradually on the horizon until it covered the full sky above me. It was a moment for reconciling with the forces of the sea. It was the moment when I merged with the ocean and lost my identity, finding a larger one, that of the whole ocean. The Milky Way appeared like a great split in the sky, like a crack in dry earth. It seemed the point of our universe's expansion towards another, more distant universe. I had the feeling that the evening, with its calm, affable nature, could tame even the sea's raging, and everything, even at the end of my most terrible days, took on a certain mildness. The night hid everything, even fears. In the semi-darkness, I stopped watching the sea and started to feel it. I felt it with the blade of my oars, with the waves lapping against my boat's hull. The sea became immaterial, lost its original consistency, becoming an emotion in which I was enveloped. In that magical atmosphere, I found ease and became more introspective. I let my gaze slide over the waves, tinged gold by the last reflections of sun. While my thoughts dug through my memory, looking for pieces of my life gone by, forgotten, plumbing its depths, and bringing back up smells, voices, and emotions. No one could ever take this beauty away from me or take away this light shiver I felt when the sea and I became one.

They say that the Greek philosopher Diogenes lived in a barrel and the only thing he had was a cloak and a water bag. One day Alexander the Great came to him, decked in all his splendor. The commander told him to ask for one wish and Diogenes answered, "Leave me my sun." It was all he needed to be happy. In these moments, I felt kind of like him, happy with little.

Yet, there were more than a few times that the sea roared like a waterfall. I was overwhelmed by the powers of nature. At those times, at night I couldn't hide my fears. They were like predators released from their dens to go on the hunt. They were irrational, uncontrollable fears. The sea often enveloped me completely. On the darkest nights I was submerged in the white, foamy water. Luckily the heavy load of food was always an excellent ballast preventing dangerous capsizing. The boat bore the sea's pressure. The wind howled like a wolf and, crouching in my little shelter, I prayed I would survive. The roar of the powerful waves that beat against my boat was so frightening that it took my breath away. I felt the impact inside my chest.

Every time a wave smashed into it and my boat survived it, I felt a burst of joy. "All right, sweetheart, come on, we can do it!" I'd yell. I slept little on those nights, both because it was hard to relax and because it was important for me to be ready for each wave to counteract its impact with the weight of my body. I'll never forget the feeling of disorientation, isolation and the endlessness of those hours. I talked to myself, stuttering when I was shaken violently. I wondered if this was really the most fulfilling way to live my life. I thought of Francesca and the nights she'd spent alone and those still to come for her. I thought of all the times she would have wanted me by her side at moments of sadness or happiness. I lingered over her pictures up in my cabin, remembering perfectly the delight of touching her skin or seeing her burst into laughter. That was what I missed. The warmth of a family and the comforting feeling of having her near.

Even something simple like making a meal could be dangerous in some circumstances. One day I was cooking pasta and I held the gas stove between my feet and with both hands I tried to keep the pan balanced, following the boat's movements. A wave made me lose my grip on the pan and most of the boiling water ended up on my ankles, giving me minor burns.

June was full of heavy rains. When the weather cleared up, it seemed like there was something different in the air. I don't know how to describe it. They were just impressions. From then on, there were many days in which I was surprised by the wind from the north or west, actually very rare in these areas. The sky was often smudged with high layers of clouds that heralded the coming of rain. The sea was not as it had been. With growing concern, I stopped to look at it. Like a soothsayer consulting his oracle, I concentrated on imperceptible changes of color and sound. I thought I could read it by now. Maybe it wasn't just a silly fancy. Maybe that long period of living with the sea in such close contact had made me able to read signs between the waves that said a lot about future conditions. With that sudden change, I started to be very afraid, but I didn't know of what. I was no longer calm. I was so focused on what was going wrong that I hardly noticed that I was still making great progress. It seemed to me that all of the sudden the sea had turned cruel and wanted to make me suffer. I became superstitious. I started to believe in the influence of nature on my life and became totally obsessed by numbers. I looked for them in dates, in the miles I covered every day, telephone numbers, on the hands of my clock. I saw them as good or bad omens based on how these numbers repeated during the days. For example if the sum of the days, minutes and seconds on my clock was an even number, this was a good omen. If on the GPS numbers appeared that were all the same or in a logical sequence of numbers, my wish would come true. And my wish was always the same: to get to Australia safe and sound.

My clothes, T-shirts and shorts (or what was left of them because all the clothes I'd taken had been ripped to shreds by the force of the wind and the sea) took days to dry because of the high humidity. My mattress, sleeping bag and the entire cabin started to smell of mold. Soon the first black spots appeared. On my big adventure, day after day, I had lost clothes, equipment essential for navigating, ropes and even watermaker. In the end I had almost nothing, and I realized I could live with even less. The indispensable was no longer indispensable, and I could have done without it. Freeing myself of excess and living only with the bare minimum was helpful to achieve an even greater success.

I was starting to lose the habit of taking care of myself. I was losing interest in little things like taking a dip at the end of the day to release my fatigue, shampooing my hair every now and then and cleaning the cabin once a week. The cabin stank, of rot and of stale air. Water often leaked inside the hatch and gathered on the floor, a brown soup with the scraps of food and dirt that I didn't pick up anymore. It was all so demeaning. My mood worsened one day when I noticed a kind of black bubble was growing on the side of one solar panel. The plastic around it had gotten very warm. An hour later, the bubble burst and the black mark spread to about half its surface. It was the third solar panel that had stopped working. Like a domino effect, I thought it would only be a matter of days before the other panels stopped working too.

I went from highly motivated to deeply depressed. Rowing was increasingly difficult. In that period, I spent more time complaining and stuffing my mouth with food than looking for solutions. The relief from food only lasted a few minutes because it was always followed by two-fold guilt. First, because of my self-harming behavior, which could cause long-term problems for my provisions. The second guilt was for my sense of self because it was an obvious rift between my ideal image of myself and the actual image that anyone who had been there would have seen. Something was getting out of hand, but what was it? How could I avoid falling victim again to this emotional state? Faced with disappointment I always reacted harshly and in the days after, I ended up punishing myself by denying myself certain foods.

Meanwhile, I kept on making great progress. In mid June, I'd reached the 150th meridian, which was half way there. I'd left behind the infinite emptiness of the Pacific and now before my prow were thousands of hidden little coral islands. Under which of those countless, little clouds, small and motionless on the horizon, was land hiding? My curiosity was turning to impatience for my first human contact. I'll always remember one afternoon because it was the day of my first sighting of dolphins. I glimpsed a commotion in the distance between the waves and I thought they were some large dorados. There were dozens of them, maybe thirty or more, and the closer I got, the more there seemed to be. As they came close to the boat, they had started to poke curiously around it. Some of them came up to sniff my scent, almost sticking their nose out of the water, but most of them kept their distance, and went on showing off with jumps and twists.

At first, the nearness of the islands had given me a sense of safety. I am sure that my support team was relieved for the same reason. But I was actually more afraid of those pieces of land than I was of the Pacific's vastness. Some were only a few meters out of the sea and others were the size of a pinhead. Though it'd been years since I'd shipwrecked on Formentera and I had put much water between me and that frightening incident, I was still very afraid of finding myself dealing with an obstacle like that again. The coral reefs that keep the islands of the Pacific sheltered from the sea's roughness were sharp blades that could have destroyed me in an instant.

The huge mass of water pushed westward by the current and prevailing winds came to a narrowing at the channel formed by the Marquesas and Tuamotu Islands, a little more than two hundred miles wide. Until that point, the ocean had been free to roam over an enormous space. Now it was channeled in that narrow passageway by the effect of the pressure that created ideal conditions by the "Venturi effect", which caused a major increase in the current speed over the following days. It was like being astride a big horse riding westward. It was very exciting and with little effort I could easily reach speeds of more than four knots. My boat slid lightly over the water. Every oar stroke gave it strength and it seemed to appreciate the push. With every inch of my body, I could feel the ease with which it moved, like it was taking little leaps from one wave to the next. The boat and I had both gotten our faith and courage back. For a short period, weather conditions improved a lot. One day, during a lunch break, while I was trimming my beard with a Swiss army knife I suddenly shouted, "A boat!" I had been rowing for several days a few dozen miles from islands and I was quite certain that I would sooner or later have the pleasure of meeting another human being. I thought I saw a square outline breaking up the peaceful flatness of the sea, so I took up some binoculars. I shouted for joy when I realized it really was a boat. Seeing this floating object sent an electric thrill through me. It might have been the best day since I started my adventure. So I picked up my VHF radio and tried to contact the captain, adding that I couldn't believe I was talking with other human beings. All that sea that separated me from the land left behind, all that time spent in the water without seeing anyone; it was as if the world of land had disappeared suddenly. A second later, the radio scratched something. In the voices of these people there was none of the joy I felt, as if meeting a rowboat was an every day event around here. "We can't see your sail. Do you need help?"

"I'm an ocean rower. I'm going to Australia. I only have oars. No sail!" I don't think my words could have surprised them more. It was like I'd said I was traveling to the center of the Earth! We continued to talk and then they reached me. I told them a bit about my adventure. It had been a hundred and forty days since I'd left and it would be just as long until I put my feet on ground again. My words made quite an impression. Before I left, the captain came near. He wished me a safe journey home and we shook hands. His hands seemed made of pebbles with calluses as rough as shark's skin. They were so big that it would have taken two of my hands to grip one of his. That hand contained all of the hardness of the coral reef and all of the kind hospitality of the people who lived there. I had never given so much attention to a handshake, but that was my first human contact after five months of solitude. The value of this gesture was immeasurable. Then I let go of the boat, loosened the rope that held them together and the current pulled me away.

That meeting with the fishermen inspired me a lot. I'd gone from a state of total calm, almost a stupor, to a new state with my senses sharper, like I'd woken up after a long sleep. The islands around me made me think that I would soon meet others. At every noise, I took up my binoculars to scan the horizon. Less than a week later, I was surprised by an unexpected event. It was an afternoon on a very muggy day.

The sun bore down on my head like a boulder. Only a light breeze gave me any relief at all. The silence of that day was suddenly broken by the roar of small patrol airplane that flew a few hundred yards up. The roar above my head startled me. Apparently I was right under the travel route of the islands. Wow! I remember that I kept on staring at that little object as if it were the first time I'd seen a plane. Only a few minutes had passed and I heard the roar of another airplane, lower than the first and going in the opposite direction. What a coincidence. I'd been isolated for a hundred and fifty days and already two airplanes within a few minutes. Only when it flew by the third time a few minutes later did I realize that it was the same airplane as before. The airplane had started to fly around me at a low altitude. Then I went into my cabin and tried to make radio contact. The first words of the response left me speechless. Not only did the person answering know my name, he even spoke Italian. It's a prank, I thought. For a second, I even thought that Francesca was on the plane. It'd be like her to do something as crazy as that. The pilot then explained that he was French, but his father was Italian. The conversation went on for a few minutes. We talked a little about everything, from the weather forecast to his love for Parmesan cheese. He asked me what could make a person go on an adventure like mine, but I didn't have a good answer. It wasn't easy to find the words. Anyhow, I could have said to him that given that he was flying a plane right then, it was because one day someone had had the daring to start on a new adventure.

After wishing me a good journey, he vanished in a second. I stayed still and quiet until the sound of the airplane disappeared in the distance.

Time was something I never stopped much to think about. It was hard for me to realize that it was passing, which of course had good effects. For a long time I wouldn't even look at the date on my logbook. Then one day I would check it and be shocked that a month had passed. Of course, the main cause of this detachment from time was because the days and seasons were all so much like. All the hours I spent rowing were monotonous and repetitive. They were so boring that I tried every thing I could to make them go by as quickly as possible.

A bit of music definitely helped a lot. Probably the funniest thing I did was writing all the countries of the world and their capitals on notebook pages and taping them on my cabin hatch. I could easily read them while I rowed and I had memorized over a hundred fifty capitals. On board, time was really optional. Sometimes I'd laugh because I was one of the few people on earth who could allow himself the luxury of choosing time arbitrarily. On my little boat, time was that little piece of the infinite between dawn and dust. I lived completely free from any need to divide time in hours or minutes. I didn't even follow daylight savings times. I moved the hands on my clock on board when I felt like it. For me, this was priceless. On land, summer was ending and Francesca had told me that she couldn't wait to see me again. If sometimes I forgot that life continued its forward march on land, life and death, in close succession, kept me aware of change. When I returned to Aprica, I would meet Clio's second son, for whom I'd be godfather. But, I would never again see two young men who died in a car accident.

As my boat grew lighter as I ate the food, it became increasingly less stable. Stressed by the force of the waves, it was a miracle I didn't capsize in some circumstances. To avoid the worst I'd tried to place my equipment and the remaining food in the lockers, hoping that this would give me more stability. I had almost capsized many times, and one night, I did indeed end up flailing on my back. I had just fallen asleep when I heard a violent impact on the boat's left side. Before I had time to open my eyes back up and understand what the hell had happened, I had already completely somersaulted. Though the main hatch was well closed, a lot of water had gotten in and it had taken me much of that night to clean out and dry the cabin. The wave had ripped the radar reflector attached to my cabin, leaving three holes that were half an inch across, which had to be filled with epoxy putty. At the end of that tube, up until a few minutes before, there had been a small Italian flag that also served as my wind vane. The next day I replaced it with a strip of white fabric, but that fluttering rag gave my boat the air of a surrender or an entreaty, and I definitely didn't want to surrender.

It seemed that from that night on, the conditions became harsher, though it was more likely a gradual change. The wind often reached speeds of over thirty knots and formed waves almost 15 feet high, too high to risk rowing. I spent more and more days below deck, desperately gripping my para-anchor, the only thing that could keep me from drifting towards the islands, a few dozen miles away. August 28th was a terrible day. Dark, heavy clouds drifted slowly overhead on that infinite stretch, stealing the color of the sea which slowly turned lead gray. I thought again of Diogenes and Aristotle, the Greek mystics and their sense of oneness with God and the entire world. But where was my God right then? Where was the sense of oneness with nature hiding? I sure couldn't find it. At dusk I was joined by a large flock of white birds, maybe terns, who were making their way back to land. Their noise, like the chirping of a million cicadas made me tremble. It all felt like a warning: take shelter, you strange species of animal, and don't forget that's what you are!

I didn't need to be clairvoyant to see that it was going to be a hard night. It was only the beginning. Ahead of me lay much worse times.

Nothing happens by chance.

Land, September 2008

The Bora wind often makes itself felt full force in Trieste. Maybe this is why I've always been enchanted by the sound of rigging boats that, as the wind whips through the masts makes a sound like hundreds of little bells. At night, the powerful whistle of the wind still brings fantastic images to mind. I always found it a mysterious, unsettling noise.

The day when Alex had to transport the boat to Genoa to load it on the container ship, we were finishing the last tasks with the Bora blowing at 100 miles an hour. It wasn't the first time I had breathed that air gone wild, but the last tasks on the boat seemed impossible. We felt like our hands would be frozen still by the cold.

Now Alex was right in the middle of the Pacific Ocean with thirty-knot winds. Here I was afraid that this wind I'd always loved would put my husband in danger. I realized that we often don't think about numbers, power, and distance. Words are words, so thirty knots just seemed like the double of fifteen, nothing more. I wondered, do you know how long a mile can be? Endless, if you have to row all of it. Do you know how high a wave in the ocean can be? Like a five-story building. Do you know how heavy a wave can be that falls on you? Heavy enough to break a sturdy cargo ship. I had a house where I could take shelter. Alex only had a 21-foot boat. When the wind was strong, he closed himself inside and waited for it to pass. A trip on the spin cycle, in random directions, for who knew how long….

S 12° 12' – E 177° 58', September 2008

There wasn't a day of rowing in which I didn't think about the effect of my success or failure on our future. If I couldn't complete my crossing, I told myself, I would probably have to choose a different line of work, one that kept me on land. If I didn't have a good outcome I might not be able to count on the support of sponsors anymore, essential for someone like me. Honestly, I'd be ready to do any kind of work. I definitely wasn't short on ideas.

I'd always liked the idea of becoming a good ice cream maker or bookseller, for instance, maybe specializing in travel literature. I had other options. That wasn't what scared me. What I cared about most was being able to give Francesca and our family a father and a husband who was fulfilled, calm and happy with himself. This depended a lot on the success of the crossing, even though I knew there was more likelihood of not getting to Australia than of getting there. I have always been sure that we are ready to achieve great success only when we are ready to face the bitterest failures. I felt prepared for humiliating defeat, if it came. Out of fear of looking bad, or being seen as an amateur when we want to think of ourselves as professionals, sometimes we choose not to risk and avoid putting ourselves to the test. With this approach, we'll never find ourselves dealing with situations that have the potential to put our self-esteem at stake. This is very understandable. It's pure self-preservation. As I grew up, I realized that this attitude limited me to doing only things that had a high chance of success. But I didn't want to only succeed, I also wanted to try. The more time that I spent on board and the closer I got to land, the more the pursuit of success was becoming a real fixation, my only reason for being.

I deserved to get to Australia, dammit! I deserved it for the effort I'd made and to repay my entire team that had worked hard for so long. I talked about it a lot with Francesca. I confessed my fears, my anxiety about the result, the pressure I was putting on myself, the deep sense of duty that made me row when the sea forbade me. She comforted me. She said I should relax, take days off when I needed, and, most importantly, get perspective on the significance I was giving to the whole adventure. "You'll see, even in the worst case scenario, we'll figure it out." She always had the right words. She knew how to fill me with faith and optimism. Being able to rely on her support was essential for me. Despite the distance separating us, which made some of our days difficult and sad, we spent most of the time calm and happy. Our life went on like any young married couple, with the one difference that I didn't come home from work in the evenings. We were often in telepathic communication to the point that when one of us was thinking of something, the other had already done it.

After four days at stormy sea and violent winds, on September 3rd, I finally passed Eva, the southernmost island of the Tonga archipelago. This brought me to a safe position, far enough away from land. That evening I thought I saw the dark form of a small island in the distance, but low visibility, due to the many low clouds made me uncertain.

The next morning when I pulled back up the rope with the para-anchor that I had thrown in the sea to stabilize the boat the night before, I realized that the steel hook to which the anchor had been attached had come accidentally unscrewed and it had slipped away. What a disaster! This discovery was followed by a moment of great despair that put me in a disoriented state of mind. Nothing was as important as that damn object. The other two para-anchors that I'd loaded before leaving had proved inadequate for my needs. The first one was a mistake, as it was too small and only useful for slightly rough sea conditions. The second was a catastrophe because the canvas was completely ripped off by the sea's violence the first time I used it. With no way of withstanding the strong currents and Australian winds, it would be insane to go on. This could make it impossible for me to ever reach land. I felt suddenly ill. I wanted to throw up at the thought and for a few minutes I sat in my cabin to think. But my mind was in a whirl.

Calm down. Stay calm and try to think of a solution. What solution was there? I'd never get to Australia! Try, you blockhead. It won't be easy, but try, and don't give up! It was amazing how quickly I changed my perspective on the situation. It was like I was dealing with two different people. Then I started to see a glimmer of hope. I wondered if everything I caught sight of might be useful for this problem. By email, Stefano had suggested tying together two oars, attaching a rope to the center of the shafts and then throwing them in the sea. Maybe they could do the job. The strategy did work, but I only used it a few times because preparing the oars took a long time and was inconvenient. Plus I was afraid they would come loose and I could lose my oars, so I stopped doing it.

On my logbook on September 7, I noted a very strong northwest drift that had stopped me from making headway south, despite great efforts. From then on, conditions drastically worsened and that was the start of a long, very hard period. The ocean current started to go in unpredictable directions, south then east, and my daily average went from thirty miles to a paltry ten miles. I was depressed, despairing and suffering pain in my back and rear. At times I didn't feel like I had the physical or psychological strength to overcome this new, unexpected hardship. It was another in a long line of tests of character, but I had used up all my desire to fight. I just wanted to let myself go. I felt my anger growing and I also was ashamed of my cowardly reaction, because I knew this was the time to take out all of my strength. The harder I rowed, the more the sea treated me cruelly. Every mile that I gained by day was lost in the night. What made me even crazier was that as soon as I stopped rowing, to eat or for a small break, the current was so strong that it turned my boat's prow eastward and dragged me away like on a moving walkway. I'd never seen anything like it, nor felt anything more humiliating. I often shouted at the heavens with all the desperation in my heart, hoping that someone could take pity on me and stop this torture. I had to fight both against the invisible force that slid under my keel, not at all easy, plus against the frustration and bitterness of seeing the efforts of hours and hours reduced to tiny progress.

On those evenings, I fell asleep with my fists gripped tight from the muscle tension that was accumulating in my body. Now I couldn't even find peace when I was sleeping. In order to minimize the hours of drift as much as I could, I rowed ceaselessly day and night, even when my eyes started to droop and my head started to bob. Fatigue was more acceptable than humiliation. I couldn't have gone on long, but in desperation I found incredible strength and I felt a hero every time I managed to go further. I was sure that the reason for the problem was the islands around me that created whirlpools and turbulence in the water. Over ten days, what had seemed like a temporary whim of the sea became a maddeningly constant companion with whom I had to learn to live. I kept on asking Roger and Stefano what in hell was happening under my keel, but they couldn't give me good explanations either. They thought that maybe after I'd passed the Tonga archipelago, I had come into part of the Pacific Ocean with irregular seabeds, not as deep as those I'd left behind, that were full of underwater mountains and very deep ocean trenches. Such an irregular seabed caused anomalies in the regular movement of the water masses. Plus, many underwater active volcanoes heated the water and the effect of thermohaline circulation (global circulation of masses of water in relationship to their density and therefore their temperature) activated swirling currents. I'd had experience with this particular phenomenon many times. On one occasion I'd also noticed that the water's temperature shifted wildly in a period of a few minutes. This rapid oscillation in temperature was matched by an equally sudden change in the direction of the current. I was in a real mess!

My thirtieth birthday was on September 15th. It was a gray, cloudy day with strong gusts of wind that brought the icy air of the Antarctic from the south, forming a very thin layer of dusty water on the sea's surface. Despite everything, the ocean still amazed me with its magic. Like many days before, it was a day spent drifting, waiting for the sea and wind to calm down. Occasional violent downpours dumped volumes of rain that I collected in plastic bottles. It was a bit salty, but I could still use it to cook. The invisible power that had recently dragged me hither and thither gave no sign of stopping. But I'd set myself the goal of not thinking about it too much, at least for that day and enjoying my birthday as best as I could. "You're thirty now, dear old Alex!" To avoid giving into the urge to gorge myself ahead of time, I'd stashed an entire Panettone cake in the farthest part of the boat that was the hardest to reach. I had stowed it on board with the plan to eat it for my birthday. But time and humidity had made it virtually inedible. It was covered with a fine greenish layer, but I certainly wasn't in a position to complain about a little mold on my cake. At these climes, you couldn't look a gift horse in the mouth. I'd finished it all by evening.

When it got dark, the sea swelled and I got ready to spend a very rough night. On my little wind gauge on board that night I had seen the wind came to thirty-three knots. I had only fallen asleep around three in the morning, when a terrifying impact, like the force of hundred men, hit me on one side and turned me over with a very slow motion. Though I was still groggy, I clearly felt my body rolling on deck house, blows to my back and the sound of the sea and all of the equipment in the cabin jumbling together. It was dark, but flashes of light crossed my eyes and when the boat straightened, I was shaken up for a long time by the sudden capsizing. I looked at the jumbled mess as if, just then, it weren't mine, as if the man standing in the middle of the ocean weren't me. It was like I'd been hung upside down. I felt physically stuck by a force that gripped my chest and stopped me from moving. I was in one piece, bruised, but not wounded. I opened the hatch and the boat's floor was still partially covered in water that was gradually flowing out of the side holes. There was nothing left of all the equipment I had left outside. In the capsizing I had lost a few bags of garbage, a bucket, a hundred yards of rope, and a small dorado that I had caught that day, already cleaned and ready to eat. I closed the hatch and I stretched out for a few seconds, breathing deeply. In those minutes, before the release of tension made me drop into deep sleep, I thought of Francesca and all the things she kept herself from saying to me on the phone. Of all the sadness she felt and solitude she was experiencing. I thought of the time I was stealing from her. Who knows how many times she fell asleep wishing for something different from her life.

I lived the following days and weeks lost in a strange feeling as silence pervaded my little world. In the solitude of my exhaustion, I learned that silence had its own essence. There was no emptiness, but there was distance and reunion at once, the start and the end of everything. I looked at my solitary shadow stretched between two waves. I wished I could take it up from the water and hug it, tell it to keep strong, assuring it that everything would be over soon. Over the next couple of weeks, I capsized another two times. Both times the fear of drowning was so great that I was afraid I wouldn't make it home again. I got used to seeing those walls of water come towards me and over me, so much that I almost didn't even notice. I rowed even when it would have objectively been safer to stay quiet in my cabin, but I was blinded by my haste and no one could have stopped me. At times, habit could make me underestimate risk. At sea, this could be an additional risk. It was at a moment when I was distracted that a wave formed out of nothing and struck the side of my boat. I will remember as long as I live the movement of air that preceded the impact, the confusion of those instants and the image of the mass of water enveloping me. The sea was so violent that in a second I found myself thrown outside in its tumultuous waters. I'd done everything I could to resist it, clinging to the upwind side of my boat, but to no avail. When I came back up, I was floating on top of my boat that was still upside down, tossed in the waves. I turned towards the hatch and through the window I saw the equipment jumbled on the roof of the deck house. What a horrible sight. In that situation, if I'd needed to call for help, I couldn't have even done so without making the boat sink. The waves and wind made my entire boat shake, and under it the water was warm. It was as quiet as a tomb and, strangely, I felt sheltered from all dangers. I was certain I would survive. I expected to see my boat turn right side up at any moment, but many minutes had passed and my boat was still upside down. Then I made a decision and I left the upwind side and then I got the idea to use my body as a counterweight to help the boat turn back over. The boat reacted immediately and a moment later, I was already back on board. It had been touch and go, but I was still afloat.

The situation that made me fear even more for my survival happened just a little while later. The sea was, of course, still rough. That morning, I was dressing to start my day at the oars and I was hit by another very violent wave that I hadn't even seen coming. When the boat capsized, I had the hatch open and my legs were halfway out of the cabin. I wasn't fast enough to pull them back in and close the hatch, so I was completely submerged by the sea. The water came up to my waist in the cabin. That calm, flat surface, on which all kinds of things floated, reflected all of my fear. The nightmare of drowning sprang up, but for a moment that seemed a lifetime, I didn't have the heart to do anything. I was stuck motionless where I was, sitting on the watertight case of photographic equipment, with one leg raised over my head propped up to one side of the deck house and my arms spread out looking for a grip to hold onto during the capsizing. I'd hit my head against a corner and cut my forehead. I put my finger to the cut that was gushing blood and I was soon covered in it. It was a shallow cut. Things could have gone much worse. I was worried about putting my food and electronic equipment in a safe place. The silence… I remember the silence and sense of powerlessness. With a little tin pan, I'd tried to bale out the water as quickly as possible, but it took me about three hours before I got the cabin in shape. There was water everywhere in every opening and every locker inside my cabin. I threw away an entire two-pound bag of sugar, a bag of freeze-dried fruit and about two pounds of cookies and all my books. "The desalinator!" I cried with an almost resigned tone. I'd used it right before capsizing and I'd forgotten to put it back in the fore cabin. It was a moment of anguish. In my mind I went over and back over those last instants, like a broken record. That pump was the only thing on which my survival at sea truly depended! I wouldn't have bet a single penny that I would be able to get it back, but leaning outside the hatch I found it stuck in a corner of the base where I put my feet when I rowed. What a relief to hold it again!

A little later, while I was putting everything back in order and cleaning with a rag, I stopped to look at the picture of my mother that I kept in a little plastic envelope. "Where were you a second ago when I capsized?" I asked her. As if the words were said by someone else, I answered myself, "I was there with one hand to help you to turn the boat over and the other hand holding the desalinator!"

I felt like crying. I was exhausted and I didn't feel like fighting anymore. I just wanted to give in to the forces of nature, the flow of water, without resisting anything anymore. The stubborn obstinacy with which I'd opposed the sea until then was giving way to humble resignation. Then I took my video camera and recorded on a tape the deepest state of despair in my life, "I'm tired… I want to go home. I want to stretch out on the couch with my wife and not spend the rest of my life here alone because what I want isn't out here." I was laid bare before that video camera. Was this the end of it all? Or was it the start of the real trip? I raised my eyes heavenward imploring God. I wanted to have that tiny crumb of hope that would give me courage again to keep on going.

About six hours had gone by and I'd managed to save a lot of my food. But I wasn't as lucky with the two GPS and with the satellite telephones that had given no signs of life since. It was a big problem because I couldn't communicate with Francesca and my team until I got to land. If they hadn't heard from me, they might think the worst. My wife isn't a fearful person who gets worried for no reason, but she would soon be wondering what had happened to me. I started to talk to her in a whisper, "Fra, don't worry. Everything's okay. I'm safe and I'm okay." I repeated the same words dozens of times in the hopes that my message would manage to fly over that mass of water and reach Francesca.

Sydney, November 2008

Macquarie Square, fortieth floor. From the office I was given to use by the Italian Institute of Culture, I could glimpse a small part of the ocean beyond the roofs. On more than a few occasions I stopped to consider that I would eventually see Alex appearing on the horizon from that direction.

I had gotten to Sydney on the morning of November 5th. A few hours later I was welcomed by the Consulate and the Italian Tourism Office to plan Alex's arrival in Australia. The welcome I got showed me right away how much excitement his adventure had stirred here too. I had the help of the entire staff of the Italian Institute of Culture to best organize the event. I had to take care of all the details of locations, local sponsors, the press, customs and quarantine procedures. I wanted his welcome to be perfect. In the best-case scenario, his crossing would have been completed by mid November. But unfortunately the winds and currents that Alex found himself facing meant I had to spend long days alone in Australia.

I talked to Stefano and Roger every day about the weather conditions. I found great support too from expert sailors and local meteorologists who were very surprised by the anomalous conditions at this time of year. Summer was making us wait for its arrival with continuous days of cold wind from the south and west. The bad weather just wouldn't make way for the good and the currents that would have helped his rowing. The days kept on being cold and windy. This meant Alex literally had to fight against the elements to try to cross the miles that still separated him from land. These were really exciting days, organizing the much awaited moment when I would hold my husband again in my arms, back from an undertaking that was truly gargantuan. This is why I was here, to be able to lose myself in his eyes that I hadn't seen for more than nine months. But my excitement was tamped down by the constant delays.

By being in Australia, at least I had the luxury of being able to see the sun set at the same moment when Alex saw it, which let me feel that he was truly close to me. I'd never given importance to the miles that separated us because I knew he was with me in everything I did. But now that those miles were decreasing I felt a sense of relief and more peace. During my days in Sydney, we'd allowed ourselves more phone calls. Lunchtime was always the nicest. In the office, everyone went out for a break and I closed myself in my room and sent some text messages to Alex. It was our time alone when no one else was around and we could take a moment just for us. But on November 11th, unlike every other day, I didn't receive any answer to my many text messages. Strange. That's not like Alex, I kept on saying to myself. I checked his position constantly on the web site to see if I saw something unusual, but he was moving towards the coast at a good speed. Alex was in an excellent position and seemed to have found currents that were taking him towards land. In those moments, it was really hard to stay calm and not let myself be attacked by anxiety, in the end I couldn't avoid it. I started to call again and again like a maniac, but I always got the same recorded voice that said the person I was trying to call was not available. Though I never thought, even for a second, that something irreversibly bad had happened, I spent a few agitated hours and hoped that Alex could contact me soon. I told myself that maybe the line was damaged, or that there was little coverage for the satellite network. I wanted to believe that Alex was fine. I needed to believe it. I had lived with this firm belief for nine months. I couldn't let myself go and give in just then. I had to be clear-eyed and present to be able to handle any kind of situation. 0088163154… I dialed Alex's number ceaselessly. As soon as I heard the automated voice, I hung up and redialed, as if I were hoping this would bring his phone back to life. Just one ring would have been enough, a text message to assure me he was OK.

Eighteen hours had passed since the last time I'd talked to him. I tried to imagine all of the possible situations he was in. Some were terrifying. Maybe his boat had capsized and he hadn't been able to right it and now he was fighting to survive.

Then I thought maybe he had just had some silly problem with his electronic equipment. I was alone and it was hard to hold in my anxiety… I called my mother in the middle of the night, pretending like nothing was going on. But she guessed from my first words that I wasn't telling her everything. After a few minutes, I dropped the charade. In Australia, it was six in the evening and with a coolness that surprised even myself, I said, "It will be dark here soon. If I send an SOS now they would wait until the morning to start to search the sea." If something had happened to Alex, they wouldn't find him. I'd said these words with shocking clarity. Despite my anxiety, one thing gave me relief: if something had actually happened to him, at least it happened while he was doing something in which he believed.

Thinking back on those moments I can see that my attitude might seem hard, but it was actually full of respect for what Alex was doing. If I never saw him again, I would be left forever with an image of him at peace with himself. I tried to call him all evening. Finally, at around ten, from the other end of the telephone, I got to hear his voice again.

"Hi, sweetheart, you can't imagine what happened to me…" From the tone of his voice, I realized he was a bit shaken up. I capsized with the hatch open. My cabin flooded and I've been trying to dry the satellite phone for hours in hopes of being able to call you."

"Tell me how you are. Tell me you're okay!"

"Only a few bruises here and there, nothing serious," he said, adding, "It was really terrible…"

I listened to him carefully while he tried to tell me what happened. He couldn't have even begun to imagine how much relief the sound of his voice gave me. The line was choppy and I was terrified that it would drop forever. He told me he was sad about the situation and felt guilty for what he'd put me through. "There will be more rough times from now on and you don't deserve it… I'm afraid communication will be difficult until I get there," he added. This threw me into despair and I wondered how I could manage without talking to him in the coming weeks. "Fra," he continued, "I promise that it will be only a few days and then we can forget it all. Forgive me for the pain that…"

These were the last words I heard him say aloud.

The microphone never worked again after that.

S 26° 03' – E 158° 26', November 11, 2008

The call with Francesca was cut short, leaving the bitter taste of unspoken words in my mouth. The telephone stayed on, but nothing was on the display and the keys no longer worked. I called her back many times, without any luck. In the following days, I tried drying both telephones. Though voice communication never returned, I at least fixed the keyboard and system for sending text messages and email.

This new disaster was a good thing if you looked at it in a certain light. It was a stroke of luck because it filled me with anger and a huge desire to take revenge on this misfortune. I got back my fire to keep on pushing, which had disappeared for a bit. I didn't want to give up because, if I did, all the effort made up until then would be for nothing and no one would know how close I got to success. I soon convinced myself that if I wanted to I could still do it. To this day, as I write these words, I can't explain who or what gave me this courage. I found my own desire to endure moving. I made a promise to myself. It no longer mattered how it ended, but as long as I was on that boat I would do everything I could to get to Australia.

I survived! The more blows I took, the stronger I got. It was enlightening to feel the stoic calm and ability to endure in the face of these adversities. It was then that my life stopped being one and the same as my goals. I was no longer them. I recognized, and only now accepted, that the force of things often carried our lives in unexpected directions. I took each day as it came. I no longer complained. I often felt like I was rowing for nothing. Until recently, this had driven me crazy, but now I had started to see everything in a different light. Though perhaps every oar stroke wasn't matched by much real progress, I somehow felt that each one was bringing me towards a new goal, a more distant goal that had nothing to do with Australia. Until that day, I had often found myself spitting at the sea, wanting to hit it right in the face. I was driven by a long-repressed rage and had even gotten to the point of throwing my own excrement in the water as a sign of disrespect. I had tried to provoke it, showing it every part of my body, insulting it and cursing it. Why was it doing this to me? What had I done to deserve this? This crazy sense of omnipotence, concealing the fear of being no one and worth nothing, was contrasted by a new side of myself that was ashamed of these bursts of rage. The sea and nature take their way and we can't imagine that we can change the wind's direction. So why did I curse myself then? I didn't want to throw in the towel. I wouldn't get off of that boat as long as I could row, but now I humbly accepted its power and its presence as something inevitable. For once, I accepted not being a hero or a champion, but just a mere man fighting with all his strength. Doing so, I gave myself back my humanity. I was finding out that the biggest challenge was less surviving the perils of the sea and more surviving myself, with that furious part that wanted to overcome every limit at any cost and the opposite side that realized that there are some limits that should be left untouched.

Since the day I'd left, the sea had fed me, slaked my thirst, kept me company, and embraced me in its immense spaces. It had made me dream of and want new journeys, growing and maturing more than I thought possible. It had made me feel like a small man, alone and faraway from everyone, while it had given me the pleasure of finding myself in the center of the universe. It had let me become the man I was.

For the entire length of the crossing I had had a lot of faith in being able to get to Australia by late November. But as that deadline was growing near, I was less certain of making it by then. There were still seven hundred miles to go, but, for a long time, I hadn't been covering more than fifteen miles a day. Since September, my progress had often been slowed by the current pushing against me. I started to think with increasing dread of the outermost date of late December. Roger, Rick, Stefano, and I had all agreed that I absolutely had to be on land by the end of the year to avoid the danger of hurricanes.

Without being able to talk on the phone, I spent a lot of time in silence. I was increasingly fascinated by the feeling of being surrounded by silence. Every now and then I would stutter a few words or sing some verses of a song, but I'd lost all interest in filling that space left by silence. Life on board was reduced to a sorry repetition of eating, resting, and rowing. I spent my days mostly sitting, sometimes in the cabin, sometimes on the seat. The muscles in my legs were greatly affected by the lack of movement. Sometimes I had to hold on to a railing when I walked. For eight months, I hadn't taken more than forty steps a day. Soon I would have to find myself an alternative that would let me get in shape for the last push. I remembered how on ships in past eras, a long trip could break the morale of the crew. If their bodies couldn't get regular physical exercise, they could grow weak. It wasn't uncommon for some captains, like Captain Cook and Shackleton, to require their men to dance or make up plays. Following their example, I started to do some motor exercises with my legs, muscle stretches, little jumps, and in my free time, I walked up and down the small deck. Plus I shouted out loud to get rid of accumulated stress. I soon felt the benefits for my body and my mood.

Good days continued to be interspersed with terrible days. Some days the air was so icy cold that I had to row in long sleeved clothes, a jacket and a hat. On others, the sun and humidity were so oppressive that I took off everything and rowed naked. The glare of the sun often burned my eyes and the salt water caked on my skin, which had started to look like cardboard. Even though I kept on slathering on the highest level of sunscreen, one day in early November, I burnt my neck and shoulders. On November 2, I passed the Continental Shelf under which Australia has jurisdiction two hundred miles from land. On that same day, Roger announced my arrival to Australian authorities. I had traveled around the world for over seventeen thousand miles. My boat had passed lands, continents, peoples, and ways of life completely different from my own, yet without my being able to know even the smallest part of them. I had left Peru many months before and now I was in Australia.

When I thought about it, I couldn't believe it.

Occasionally I still caught some fish on my hook, mostly dorados. One night, not long before going to sleep, I saw a dozen of them who were munching on the barnacles stuck to my hull. I managed to catch a very big one. I cleaned it and left it in a bucket outside of my cabin. I went to bed, but the thought that birds might steal it made me decide to stash it in my cabin. During the night, the bucket turned over, and it was a long time before I got rid of the nauseating stench of fish. I had gradually lost all pleasure and curiosity for anything that wasn't essential for my survival. On good days, Australia seemed just around the corner. On not so good days, it grew distant from my thoughts and I went back to being a small man lost in the middle of the sea. Every evening, before I fell asleep, I counted the miles that I still had to go to land. For weeks, the count had stayed almost the same. Yet, every morning, something pushed me to get on that damn seat.

S 26° 27' – E 160° 07', December 2008

Every now and then I looked around me and felt overcome by doubt and fear. All it took was a slightly darker cloud, a stronger gust of wind, a certain ocean condition for me to feel my soul in pain. The closer I got to land the more this feeling grew. It seemed directly connected to the fear of making a mistake at the last moment of the crossing. The fewer miles to land, the smaller the margin of error. The outcome depended greatly on many factors at the same time, like the weather, the currents, and my position. The narrower these parameters grew, the less chance for a positive outcome there was. Fueling this state of mind and making me even more suggestible, on dark, stormy nights, it seemed like the wind was carrying voices that shouted my name: "Aleex… Aleeex…" More than once I almost went out of the cabin to answer. I never managed to get used to the long series of noises that the boat made as its constant swaying spread them everywhere. The clicks and hisses of moving objects, the creaking of the seat, shots and bursts, dripping water, the murmur of the wind, and the constant background noise of the sea. I never had nightmares. I dreamed a lot, mostly situations at sea, except for twice. In the first dream, I was walking in the darkness and was suddenly attacked by a tiger that jumped out of nowhere. But instead of being afraid, I managed to catch it by its neck and wrestle it to the ground. In the second one, I dreamed of rowing on gravel, surrounded by bushes and trees. The sound of a little stream was in the distance. I continued with great effort, but I was very optimistic because I thought that with the coming of high tide, the sea level would increase and I would be able to go again.

On December 3, the current brought me to the peak of an underwater mountain, immersed a little more than 3,000 feet under the sea's surface. The extremely powerful whirlpool made around this enormous mountain went clockwise and forced me to follow it. I was carried eastward at four and half knots. I had never reached this speed rowing. Before giving into the current I had tried strenuously to fight it, but after a whole day spent tiring myself out, I couldn't even get a mile in the direction I wanted. To reach Australia I would once again have to accept being pulled away from it first.

According to the data collected by Roger and Stefano, we could expect that the current coming from the eastern part of the mountain to turn southwest and then west, returning me to my course. The big oval merry-go-round would take about a week to bring me back to where I'd started. Though it was a week thrown away, at least I could breathe a big sigh of relief. It was all still possible. I just needed patience. What a joke on me though! Even smack in the middle of the Pacific, it was a mountain that caused me the biggest problems. One mountain attracts the other, I thought. While I was going on this spin, another guy from Valtellina like me was having a rough time because of another mountain, much larger and more forbidding. My friend, the mountain climber Marco Confortola, was recovering from an attempt to climb K2 that ended in tragedy. It was now three months later, and he had yet to recover fully. In April, we'd talked a couple of times when he was working on installing a weather station on Everest, the highest in the world.

One night, I was woken by the phone ringing. "Hello?"

"Dude… how you doing?" his voice was unmistakable. With his expedition partner Silvio Mondinelli, he was in Camp 2 in a tiny tent, chattering his teeth from the cold while a blizzard roared outside. He was breathing heavily and coughing repeatedly. At those altitudes, you got tired even just standing still in a tent. It was a funny phone call because each of us laughed at the misfortune of the other. I was in the sweltering heat and frying my brain and he was in the Himalayan cold, turning into an icicle. Two worlds so far apart, two lives lived at opposite extremes, yet so much alike.

"You know, Alex, wouldn't we be better off just staying at home?

"No, Marco, we wouldn't be better off at home and you know it! Maybe we'd be more comfortable, that's true, but it wouldn't be enough for us. You're there and I'm here because that's what we want!"

In July, Marco had left to take on K2, but then there was no way to talk on the phone. Occasionally his brother Luigi send me short text messages. On August 2, he told me that Marco, after reaching the peak, had run into some problems and that for twenty-four hours he was stuck at the eight thousand meter altitude, trying to rescue some Korean mountain climbers who were stuck upside down in a serac. Everyone feared the worst. Not many mountain climbers had survived so many hours beyond the "dead zone". But with his great stubbornness and sense of duty, he succeeded in his attempt to reach them, and sadly, despite it all, he found them dead. He had suffered serious frostbite on both feet. A month later, surgeons were forced to amputate all ten toes of his feet. The biggest adventure for him had just started.

Meanwhile, the sea and wind had done with me as they pleased for three weeks. I had tried to do everything I possibly could. I had found and lost the right current dozens of times, wandering desperately every which way in the ocean's expanse, like trying to catch a wild hen in a chicken coop. Stubbornly, I spent many days and nights trying to catch it, changing direction every time Roger or Stefano told me of a new chance to catch it somewhere else. I wouldn't give up. I was sure that I would get to land on my own strength if I could just keep up that attitude. Yet there were more than a few times that I wondered if I would see this in a different light years down the road. Is it always right to keep on going? Up to what point is it worth it? Even though I considered myself kind of crazy and though all of that hardheadedness verged on the absurd, every night when I finally put down my oars and went to sit in my cabin, I thought it was the only thing I could do because, in the end, that's why I was there. I no longer rowed to reach land, but to make sure I always kept the right to be the person I was. Sometimes I felt deep frustration, but I lived my days with hope and a positive attitude, managing to row without thinking of the result anymore, but just for the sake of rowing. Finally I got back that lightness of living that had been with me on the first part of the crossing. I wrote in my logbook, "The fastest way to end a war is to lose it." This had become my personal mantra to perseverance that I repeated to myself out loud every time that discouragement set foot on my boat. Because I couldn't do more than I was doing, I became deeply fatalistic. I passed New Caledonia, where southeast winds held me in check for many days, making me even consider having to land on its coasts. Finally I saw the great continent of Australia before me. Right then, I felt that nothing and no one could stop me from getting to Australia. Every evening I obsessively looked at the pilot chart with which I had marked my progress every month. I felt deep satisfaction at seeing how little was left now. In those moments of deep fulfillment, it was so real that I felt like I could touch my dream with my fingertips. I saw that I was really almost there. It was hardly 3/4 of an inch on the map!

It had been a month since I had seen the first pieces of land close up, on October 16. They were the Matthew and Hunter islands, which were volcanic formations of two conical islets, both rocky and yellow from ancient lava sulfur. The morning that I woke up to see them before me was pure elation. I was still more than a thousand miles from the coast, but suddenly it was like this sight of land would give me a push to cover the distance in a single bound.

Bad weather kept on returning regularly and not being able to ever say, "OK, I'm done for the night!" I was exhausting myself. The thought of losing miles already crossed pushed me every night to spend less hours resting and more rowing. Every time that bad weather forced me to stay in my cabin looking at that old, rusty sliding seat and those oars that looked like stumpy wings, the boat left to its own devices, I thought that I would never make it to land and was in desperate need of help.

I started to pray with such continuous fervor that the only words in my mouth were addressed to God.

Francesca had already been in Sydney for thirty days to organize my arrival. She had met with the Water Police, the immigration office, customs, the Italian Consulate, and the great number of people who supported me from Australia. She had made agreements with TV, journalists, and photographers. Everything was ready for my arrival. We were already imagining the party that our large Italian community had organized at the Opera House in our honor. It hadn't been easy to get the permit to row inside the bay of Sydney to the Opera House and we had to accept adhering to strict rules. One of these restrictions was that once the mouth of the bay was reached, I was required to be accompanied by a ship of the Australian coast guard to the immigration office where I would go through customs procedures. They were very exacting instructions. No food on board. No medicine and no animals, living or dead, on my boat, and the hull had to be cleaned of the incrustations that had grown at high sea. No closer than twelve miles from land, I had to empty all of the lockers of seawater. This was all to protect Australia's biodiversity. Then, still escorted by the police, I could reach the final jetty.

On December 12, just forty hours after the last weather report by Roger had encouraged me to take advantage of particularly favorable sea conditions, Francesca wrote me a long email in which she described a situation that was quite dramatic and very different than the one described by Roger's weather report. It was an emergency report sent to all harbor masters of New South Wales about a very rough sea with eastern winds over forty knots. That wasn't all. Soon the wind would turn from the east and push me at least a hundred miles back out to sea. I spent all of that night at the oars. I could barely see the full moon through the layer of clouds. There wasn't a lick of wind. The landscape was infused with a strange, supernatural calm. In brief moments, the moon reflected on the sea surface and I could see the long wake of my boat splitting the water like a blade. I was playing my last cards all in a few hours. When the sun rose I realized that I hadn't made the progress I hoped. I started to prepare myself psychologically for another difficult day. From my first oar strokes, I realized that I wouldn't have enough time to cover the miles left to go to land before the wind turned, even in the best case scenario. I had to do about thirty hours for seventy miles. Maybe I could make do with less, fifty or sixty to get to an area protected enough from the wind to avoid the worst conditions. Only two options were left. The first was to cross my fingers, face the bad weather, as I had many times before and see what happened. But it would be a huge risk. The other, more responsible, option would be to take advantage of the lucky coincidence of a New Zealander tow boat that was making its way from New Caledonia to the town of New Castle, a hundred miles north of Sydney. In about eight hours, it could bring me to land.

In favor of the second option was another factor to take in account; it was possible that the weather would end up forcing me to abandon my boat in the sea. No one would have taken the risk of getting it to land in stormy sea conditions. How much would it cost me to be myself right then? Maybe even my life. I didn't want to risk losing it for any adventure in the world.

There are moments in a person's life in which our life his no longer our own. There are moments when our very ambitions, the desire to go further, force our hand. But, if there was ever a moment when I felt truly at the helm of my life and with total control of all the forces that drive me, it was when just sixty miles from land, I decided to stop.

That final choice, so unusual for me, made a big impression on Francesca too, who would have never expected it. There were two very hectic hours and at one in the afternoon, in a sea about to swell, I glimpsed a small boat nearing. It was the *Katea*, the tow boat that would bring me to land. About two hours later I stepped on board.

I could never explain, in any book, or in any language, how hard it was to make that decision. It was devastating, as if someone had suddenly taken away all my certainties and everything I had, but it was never, in any way, humiliating. Those sixty miles on board of the *Katea* taught me much more than ten thousand miles of rowing had. I can say without question that this was the finest success of my life.

Land, December 12, 2008

"Are you at peace with it?" Just a few minutes after Alex decided to end his crossing, I wrote him this message on his satellite phone. I was exhausted. I hadn't been able to communicate with him by voice for forty days and I just wanted to hear the tone of his voice to understand if his decision was taken peacefully. A few seconds later, I received a message and my heart started to beat like crazy: "Yes. I have everything I need to be happy. It's really over, my love!"

New Castle, December 13, 2008

The *Katea* reached the port of New Castle just after nine in the morning. The arrival was planned for six in the morning, but bad weather that night had forced the captain to keep to a low speed and caused a delay of several hours. I recognized land from afar just as I came up from below deck and I glued my eyes to it and never looked away again. Only when the last rope was tied to the bollard and the boat was moored to the dock was Francesca allowed to come to me. I couldn't go on land yet because I first had to go through the controls of immigration and custom's agents. A large group of people formed around us, including journalists, photographers, and curious onlookers, but we'd been waiting for this moment for such a long time that it felt like we were the only two people there. I buried myself in her hair and smelled her scent and felt her breath on my neck. It was only then that I really felt the distance that had separated us and I realized how horribly much I'd missed her. For a few moments we couldn't even speak a single word. She was the first to speak, "I'm so proud of you!" I wanted that moment to last forever.

The first days on land were a whirlwind of emotions. Walking around Sydney, I was recognized and stopped by people of all nationalities, who all wanted to congratulate me for my adventure. The day after my arrival at the Opera House a welcome event was organized, and I met a huge number of people who came to celebrate with me. A band of all Italian immigrants played the Italian anthem for us. I was in a daze. My ears rang like after a bomb explosion. But I was happy. Very happy.

In Italy I was welcomed with just as much warmth. I was very pleased that thousands of people had followed me every day. What bothered me a little was the importance some people gave to the unlucky end of my adventure. As if everything I had done before the day I got on the *Katea* tugboat was suddenly null, a negligible detail. It's not that I wanted credit for something, but I was completely unprepared to talk about my adventure from the banal perspective of a failed record attempt. For me, it'd been a positive life experience, an extraordinary trip that had given me infinite emotions and taught me enormous lessons.

At any rate, three days after I got to New Castle, the Ocean Rowing Society, an English association that certifies rowing crossings, had made the positive outcome official.

This detail doesn't add anything to my adventure because what matters to me is something else entirely. But people still stop me and say, "Alex, I'm sorry. What a pity. You almost did it!"

"Almost did what?" I always wondered. I had almost managed to kill myself, sure, but I stopped just short of it to come home safe and sound. Every time I have to explain again that Australia was my arrival point, but my goal was to cross the Pacific, which I did. And the end, though it may not have been what I'd dreamed, was the best thing that could have happened to me in my life. It was the best thing for me right then.

Sometimes when we are near reaching a big goal, we see ahead of us the line that goes to our target. We want to devour it with our eyes. We have worked so hard to get to that point and now that line is ours and no one can take it away from us. We want to get to that target at any cost. After having chased land for almost three hundred days I was tired, overwhelmed, hungry, bent by fatigue, but I had enough strength left in my mind and body to reach Australia and go beyond. If my life hadn't been at stake I would have dared to go on and maybe I would have reached land. Destiny often prevails over our dream, and unexpected events can block the road at the last minute. It is at that moment that we have to have the humility to recognize our powerlessness.

More than in any other adventure before, in this one in the Pacific, there were very many days in which I was overcome by uncertainty about the future, doubt, and fear. Years before, I might have rejected or denied myself these states of mind. But now I look at them in the face and I am no longer afraid of them because I think they are essential for my growth and development. This fills me with pride today. Sometimes it is very easy to win, easy to be proud of ourselves when things go well and we ride the wave of success. It's not as easy to keep the same pride when we suddenly have to deal with a personal setback, whether small or large. It is precisely in that moment, when everything is falling apart and we feel overwhelmed by an insurmountable sense of nothingness, and we are blind with rage, that we have to prove to ourselves our courage to look reality in the face. Maybe after some time has passed, we can even realize that not reaching our target was a great stroke of luck.

We are the children of a society that puts out of proportion emphasis on the idea of success and denies or hides everything that doesn't fit with this. I don't like that at all. I want to be an example against the grain. I want to show the educational value of falling down and failures, of all those times that we aren't champions. We have to teach our children, before teaching them to fight to win, to fight to live, to not be afraid to dare. We have to teach them that the value of a person is not measured by the number of times he or she climbed to the top of the podium, but how many times after a fall, that person got back up and said, "Let's go!"

I don't think I did something so exceptional in the crossing. Of course, it might make people curious, but I was just trying with all I had to follow my instinct as a person and realize my dream. There is nothing exceptional in this, though I realize that sometimes living your dreams or trying to make them come true is exceptional in itself because it is the most difficult and complicated thing in the world. Each of us has our own oceans to cross, challenges to overcome, moments of despair that annihilate us and moments of victory that make us feel like a lion. All of us should be aware of the enormous potential of human beings.

In the Pacific, as in the Atlantic, my motto, written in indelible letters on my boat's cabin was: "Onward, bastard," a message that often gave me the grit I needed to overcome my difficulties. These are the only words I want to remember.

"Onward, bastard!

Aprica, December 12, 2009

The day you came through the door of our house our lives were changed forever. In the nine months of waiting, your mother and I often stopped to think of the time we would hold you. But the emotion that you give us every time we see you make a little grimace or the hint of a smile is beyond anything we could have imagined. You know, even when you cry, and sometimes you cry so much that your chin trembles and your face turns beet red, I think you're the most beautiful thing in the world. It's so strange to think that a little more than a week ago you weren't here yet, or rather you were an idea in our minds, not yet with your identity. I didn't know anything other than that you got mad when we played at wrestling. Sometimes your mother's belly suddenly popped out on one side on the top. I thought that it was one of your little feet, I tried to push back on this first expression of strength and you responded with some kicks. You were so funny. Now I look at you and I feel like I've known you forever. We had the confirmation that you were definitely our daughter during the last gynecological visit before you were born. Your birth was expected from around November 20th, but on the day of that visit, the 26th, you hadn't given any sign of being ready to be born and we were calling you lazy. The midwife said that you had your head looking upwards. "This baby girl likes to look at the stars," she said. With two parents like us, you couldn't help but have your eyes on the sky.

As you grow up, Sofia, try to hold on to this habit of looking skywards. Have high expectations of yourself, but when you make a mistake, know how to give yourself a second chance. Keep your curiosity and your interest in simple things alive, and never settle for mediocrity. Try alternative routes, learn to look at things from different perspectives and always have the courage to take your own paths. Be true to yourself, but accept changing your objectives when you need to. Accept the consequences of your choices and keep on acting and fighting for your right to dream to be respected. It won't be easy. You will have to be determined and soon you will learn that living freely takes a huge dose of responsibility. But it is always worth it.

While I am writing the last lines of this long story, I am watching you sleep and I understand the great luck I've had. Who knows how many times before you go to sleep, I will tell you the story of the whales or the stinging jellyfish or the bird that perched on my head? Who knows how many times you'll say to me, "Papa, you've already told me that a thousand times."? By the way, did I ever tell you the time at sea on day, looking at the clouds that I saw one that looked like a fetus? Clouds are beautiful because they take the form of whatever we are imagining.

I don't know what will happen from here on out. Maybe one day I will go again on a new trip to bring you home another story to tell. We will spend periods far apart, but I want you to know that there will never be a day when I don't think of you and your mom. You two are my best adventure. Every departure will have its return. I hope that each time I come back I can be a person who is a little better than when I left.

I am leaving this last page blank so you can start from here and write the extraordinary story that will be your life.

Love, Papa

Acknowledgments

The story of this adventure could not have been told without the support of my ground team, which included Roger Stewart, Stefano Martini, Cristiano Baroni, Dr. Alberto Zoia, Dr. Giulio Rossi, director of the sports medicine center at the Morelli hospital in Sondalo, and Gianluca Farina for his indispensable advice as technical expert of the Italian National Rowing team.

Silvano Piana, who deserves special thanks for his faith in me, as long as two oceans, and the sponsor Findomestic Banca.

Massimo Cirri and Filippo Solibello who, through Radio2's Caterpillar program, made me feel close to land.

The thousands of people who supported me, encouraged me and even criticized me through the web site.

The Italian Culture Institute of Sydney, the Italian Consulate, the Foreign Trade Institute, and the National Tourism Office.

All our friends in Australia and, before that in Italy, who supported Francesca during her long wait.

To my friends Clio, Ale, and Ivano.

Francesca, my wife, for knowing how to go across an ocean with me.

And, of course, Manuela La Ferla for her patience and the Longanesi publishing house for giving me this chance again to tell about my adventures.

For the English version thanks to Miriam Hurley for her great professionalism in translation. I want to express my gratitude for her having taken, with dedication and passion, the challenge of understanding the feelings hidden behind the words.

My most sincere thank goes to all the people who has supported the crowd-funding campaign by which the digital version of this book has been published. I will be forever grateful to Lorenzo Paoli, Benedetto Latteri, Alejandro Funicic, Matteo Torretta, Riccardo Rodella, Lia Coloni, David Antoine,

Stefano Martini, Antonio Poloni, Paolo Ferrari, Lorena Cremonesi, Barbara Burns, Alessandro Palmieri, Jeffrey Perrella, Julian Crabtree, Pietro Pollichieni, Nino Bellini, Fabio Mangiarotti, Mirko Visentin, Laura Locatelli, Francesco Tortoreto, Laureen Hudson, Alex Dixon, Simone Foggiato, Pier Francesco Verlato, Giacomo Inches, Marco Bicocchi Pichi, Carol Atkinson, Giacomo Chiozza, Naike Gualtieri, Bernadette Hansel, Gianluca Morini, Riccardo Donadon.

Appendix

How to help this book: a request

Thank you for buying this book. If it somehow exceeded your expectations or left you feeling good or, thinking that this story would be better if more people read it, this is for you.

As you know by now, I'm a young, independent author. I don't have a huge marketing machine behind me, nor a gang of billionaire friends, or even a magic genie offering me three wishes. But that's ok. If you're willing to chip in a few minutes of your time, you can seriously help this book find its way in the cold, tough world, where many good books never reach all the people they should.
Please consider doing any of the following:

- Write a review on Amazon.com
- Post about this book to your blog, on Facebook, or on Twitter.
- Recommend the book to coworkers, your friends and your friends' friends, or your friends with blog, or your coworkers' friends who blog, or even your friends of friends who blog about their friend's blogs. The possibilities are endless.
- If you know people who write for newspapers or magazines, drop them a line.
- Check out www.alexbellini.com and discover all the great things I write about each week. If you like what you find, run through this list again with that in mind.

These little things make a huge difference. As the author, my opinion of the book carries surprisingly little weight. But you, dear reader, have all the power in the world.

Not only can you help this book find its way, but you'd also make the many risks of writing the next book easier to overcome, increasing the odds that I'll do an even better job next time around.

As always, thanks for your help and support.

Alex

The departure with the city of Lima in the background.

The farewell with Francesca with the promise to meet her again soon. (photo © Reuters / Pilar Olivares).

At times the fishing was really rich …

…other times it was very poor.

My refuge, small but comfortable.

A marine animal emerges from the bottom

On the days of rest the hours passed slowly.

An unusual pair.

The encounters with the wildlife is the most exciting thing I remember.

The day of my 30th birthday. Outside the storm continued to rage.

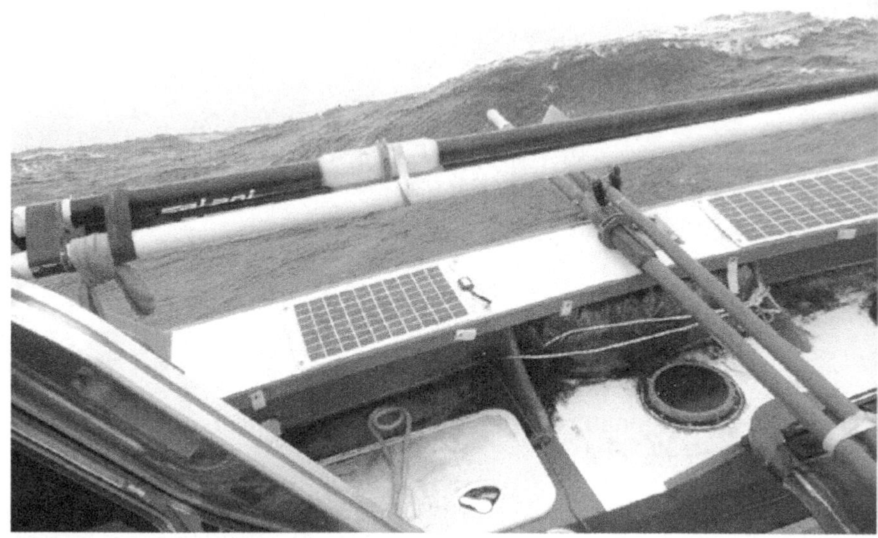

Stormy sea off the islands of Tonga

The arrival in Newcastle 294 days later (photo © Gino Nalini)

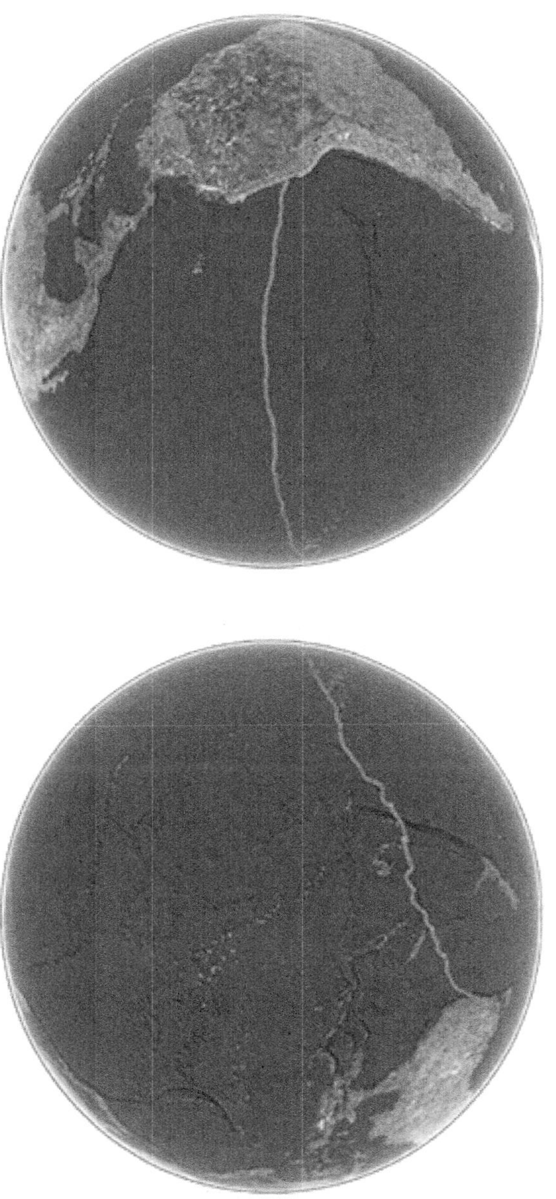

My route to the Pacific.

Made in United States
North Haven, CT
13 April 2023

35403534R00071